South Africa 1979

KEITH RICHARDSON

DEDICATION

To everyone who made this possible.
You know who you are.
Thank you.

CONTENTS

ACKNOWLEDGMENTS

I would especially like to thank the innumerable people who were kind enough to provide me with lifts, drinks, food, accommodation and their excellent company and candid observations, much fun, love, and sound advice on life during the Apartheid era.

Several maps have been sourced and accredited as required from OpenStreetMap.org, which are free to use under their open license.

Photographs are my own. Where helpful to the story a small number of additional images are included sourced from Wikipedia under their licence terms where those allow for their reuse and are accredited accordingly.

1. INTRODUCTION

Places Explored

This is the story of a surreal 10-week, 7,560-mile, hitch hiker's tour of the people and places of Southern Africa. The map below traces the routes of the various trips taken over the 10 weeks in southern Africa:

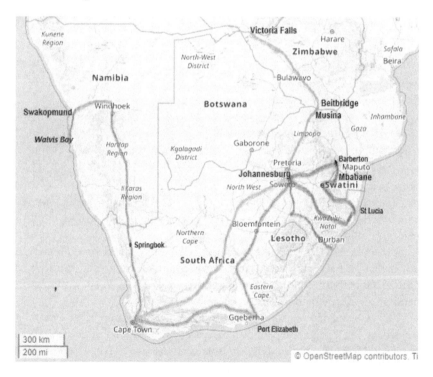

Places visited included Swaziland (now called Eswatini), South West Africa (Namibia) & Zimbabwe-Rhodesia (Zimbabwe), taking in Johannesburg, Barberton, Piggs Peak, Mbabane, St Lucia, Bloemfontein, Port Elizabeth, Garden Route, Cape Town, Windhoek, Namib Desert, Swakopmund, Walvis Bay, Springbok, Great Karoo, Britstown, Musina, Beitbridge, Bulawayo, Victoria Falls, Durban, Pretoria and innumerable places in between.

This book shares many of the surreal encounters on the cusp of immense political and cultural transition in southern Africa. To pick a small selection, they ranged from the author being likened to "Mad Dogs and Englishmen" for standing out in the mid-day sun in the Namib Desert; to sleeping in a sheep truck, to getting badly bitten by bed bugs; to taking over the driving of a smashed car after they hit a poor donkey at 75mph, to a "cowboy style standoff" with soldiers in the desert at midnight; to being handed a bag of hand grenades and pistol with the instructions that if any trouble kicked off, I had to get out of the vehicle fast, throw myself in the ditch, or bush, by the roadside, keep very low and shoot anything that moved, except him, as well as throw the grenades at "them". I also enjoyed the immense hospitality, kindness and generosity of many from all sections of society; had some of the best nights out ever at the PiG in Jo'burg, The London Town Pub in Durban, the Pig and Whistle in Cape Town, the Kalahari Sands Casino in Windhoek and the Victoria Falls Hotel. If that wasn't enough, I also had some of the most engaging discussions with members of many racial groups that make up what is now known as the Rainbow Nation, or back then, as one renowned and isolated for its Apartheid policies. And that's only a small selection.

Getting The Ducks Lined Up

It will all become clearer as the story unfolds, but starting at the beginning, back in January 1979, I'd written to my friends, Jenny and David, asking if it would be ok if I came over to see them in Johannesburg, South Africa, in the summer for a while. Then I would go off on various tours of the vast country. They wrote back in February to say, yes, that would be great if I could. It would be best to arrive early in July before David started the new university term on the 23rd July. Then they could spend some time with me when I arrived. They wrote to me again in May to say, not to worry about paying them for food and lodging, all I would need would be my spending money, which was very nice of them both.

They also warned me to "be careful of my reading matter" as I could get arrested at Jan Smuts Airport for carrying "undesirable" literature and be sent packing back to the UK on the next flight. So, no Penthouse or Mayfair magazines (for those who don't know they were known as "girlie" magazines containing scantily clad, or nude pictures of pretty women that were popular with some elements of male society back then. "They", the Broederbond, were apparently a secretive organisation of mainly Dutch descent Calvinist Afrikaner men that held many positions of power in government and effectively ran the country. They had even banned "Black Beauty" at one stage apparently. I never bought those kinds of magazines anyway, so I was going to be safe.

So, it was all systems go to try and get two essential elements into place in the next few weeks. Firstly, enough time off work to make the considerable cost worthwhile and secondly, the funding to oil the wheels of travel.

Time Off

To get the time off work was going to require considerable efforts of persuasion on my part. I only had 4 weeks annual leave in total that I had already saved up. So, I decided to apply for 6 weeks unpaid special leave to give me a generous 10 weeks in South Africa. I had to meet the Training Manager at the aerospace company where I worked to explain myself and plead my case. So, at the interview I did my best to convince him … it would give me an opportunity to see my friends, an opportunity to experience other cultures, it would be mind expanding, educational, I was not asking to be paid, I would do it in a gap between my work placement and starting back on the final year of my Business degree. So, no interruption to working arrangements, etc, that kind of thing. It worked. He gave permission. That was the first hard part out of the way.

Funding & Flight

The second part, funding, was more of a challenge. The £650 cost of a return airline return ticket from Heathrow to Johannesburg was far from cheap by the way back in 1979. That's the equivalent of about £3,360 in 2020 according to the Bank of England inflation calculator. The era of "low cost – no frills" airlines, offering low-cost flights and so on, had only just begun operation in 1977 with pioneers like Freddie Laker's Airline. Others, like Virgin Atlantic, EasyJet and Ryan Air, were still to enter the market. The internet, with rapid access to online price comparisons data, was non-existent too. So, state subsidised and protected airlines and routes were still the norm. Just to give you some idea of how much things have changed in the years since then, I bought a return ticket UK Manchester-Sydney, Australia in 2019 for £645 return. That was equivalent to £127 in 1979. Also, in May 2017 I went back to South Africa for a 16 days / 15 nights guided tour with a very respectable tour operator that cost only £1,799 in total, including UK-South Africa flights, 4-star hotel B&B accommodation throughout, all in country transportation by coach, many meals and plane. In other words, half of what I paid in 1979 in real terms just for the flights alone. I've written a book about that as well: "South Africa 2017".

My salary in 1979 was £3,000 gross pa (equivalent to about £15,500 in 2020). So that flight ticket was a 20% chunk of that, or about 30%, if you take the income tax, National Insurance, and pension contributions into account. I'd worked as a barman in the evenings at a pub near where I lived at the time, to make as much extra money as I could. That also minimised my "socialising" expenditure too because I was on the side of the bar earning it, as opposed to on the other side, spending it. That way I was able to just about afford the trip, as well as drawing on some savings from previous summer jobs. Plus, I had a new Barclaycard credit card and overdraft facility lined up just in case they were needed (which they were).

Passport and Vaccinations

I already had a passport, having been on a camping holiday to France wi6h my parents when I was 16. So that was one less expense to pay for. So, with the approval of my friends in Jo'burg, time off, money being saved and flights booked, it was time to prepare to get vaccinated. On the 12th May 1979 I had the required vaccinations at my GP's to obtain the essential International Certificate of Vaccination.

London Heathrow Departure

Well, the time flew by and on 6th July 1979 I finished my 3rd Year Industrial Apprenticeship Placement at the aerospace company as part of my 4-year Business degree. After work, I went back to the bungalow that I shared with three other young men, Andy, Martin, and Tony, who also worked at the company, and packed my things to begin my big adventure.

The following day, 7th July, I travelled down south to check in to London Heathrow airport before the 8.45pm deadline for the 9:45pm flight to Johannesburg. Those were the days before "9-11" and added security, so there was no "3 hours pre-flight arrival time" then. The plane was meant to take off at 9.45pm, but was delayed. The flight crew said it was because they couldn't get enough ground staff to put all the bags and things in the plane, or steps transported to the rear door to let everyone on, until 15 minutes before we were due to fly. Industrial relations between "management", "airlines" and "unions" weren't too good at that time apparently.

To Infinity and Beyond?

Well not quite, but I'm sure that if Buzz Light Year had feelings, he would have felt like I did at Heathrow. Excited, a little anxious, alive, and very excited. This was, after all, my first ever flight in my entire life to date and not only that, but I was flying on the biggest passenger jet at the time, a SAA Jumbo Jet (South African Airways). Exciting times!

We all eventually boarded the plane two hours later than scheduled and shortly afterwards the jumbo was pushed off the stand, the jet engines wound up and it rolled towards the runaway. I had that feeling of great anticipation that this was going to happen after all that effort and planning. The plane's engines roared to full throttle, and it rapidly picked up speed as it rumbled down the runway, picking up speed before lifting off and climbing steadily to cruise height at 36,000 feet. I had a window seat on a row all to myself and sat glued to the glass looking out at the ground moving below as clouds rushing past, eager not to miss any of it.

It didn't seem very long before the captain said, "We are now over Germany and will be arriving in Nairobi at 10am local time". The overhead light was to my right and I'm right-handed, so it was casting a pretty good shadow just where my pen was while I wrote in my diary. Back in 1979 jumbo jets did not have "back of the seat" televisions, but they did have an "audio" sound system with a selection of pre-recorded programmes I could listen to through headphones. So, I had a browse and found an audio book version of "War of the Worlds" by Jules Verne. It was beautifully narrated by Richard Burton.

Then, in the early hours, I fell into a fitful sleep of sorts, more like snoozing intermittently, interspersed by periods of star gazing when I woke as my head crashed down onto my chest. I eventually gave up trying to snooze as dawn broke on the eastern horizon over Africa and the beautiful sun rise lit the clouds and eventually the earth below. What was noticeable was that Africa was brown in colour. It was the dry season. There were a few bushfires visible too, given away by the plumes of smoke stretching out like plump duvets cast over the savannah and far up into the sky.

We arrived in Nairobi just as the captain said, at 10am. Compared to Heathrow, Nairobi Airport was tiny. It looked like they were scrimping on maintenance a little. It was a brief uneventful stay to refuel, so two hours later, we were back on board and off again. Shortly after takeoff the captain announced that the huge mountain peeking out of the sea of clouds was Mount Kilimanjaro in the Rift Valley. That was truly an amazing sight. It really was a like an island thrusting up through an ocean of cloud.

It wasn't until the captain announced that we were crossing over the Zambian border into Zimbabwe-Rhodesia that signs of large-scale cultivation and "signs of civilisation" began to increasingly replace what seemed to be vast swaths of plains and forests with little or no sign of human urban activity. The captain announced we were flying over Salisbury the capital of Zimbabwe-Rhodesia, as it was then called, then, that we were over the Limpopo River which marked the border with South Africa.

"I could have sworn it was green!"

Nearly there now I thought and so, with mounting excitement and some 14 hours after taking off from Heathrow, on the 8th of July, the flight touched down at Johannesburg's Jan Smuts International Airport. It was named after a former South African Prime Minister (now renamed O. R. Tambo International Airport). It was 2pm and my first ever flight was over. I had enjoyed the food and the service from the very helpful and attentive airhostesses who were excellent, as well as the incredible views of Europe and Africa.

After disembarking it took me 2 more hours to get through Customs because they had to process another jumbo jet full of people that arrived at about the same time, so about 600 passengers in total. Plus, I accidentally walked past the baggage carrousel where my bag was yet to pop out of and ended up walking straight through into the Customs before I realised my mistake. That presented clear evidence of my credentials as a novice sleep deprived, international traveller to the amused Customs Officers, who promptly packed me off back into Baggage Reclaim to get my bag. Well, I managed to find the correct baggage carrousel, but then I couldn't find my bag. I could have sworn it was green. I had not slept much on the flight, so I think my appalling memory recall ability was probably caused by jet lag. However, as the number of people gathered around the revolving baggage carrousel declined as they retrieved their bags and headed for the Customs area, I began to fear that my bag was in Brazil or China thanks to the Heathrow baggage handlers. Or perhaps some opportunist baggage handler or passenger had stolen it. It then dawned on me that that lonely blue bag going round and round on the carrousel looked strangely familiar and, on interception and closer inspection, I realised it was, in fact, my bag. It wasn't green, yet I was so convinced it was. So blue bag in hand, I headed for Customs again, but the Customs Officers just laughed and waved me through. Since then, I have always tied a coloured ribbon on my bag handle.

2. WELCOME TO THE LITTLE HOUSE

Black Things with Yellow Stuff

Just like in the movies, with eager anticipation, I exited into the reception area and there were my friends, Jenny and David, waiting for me. They were pleased to see me, and I was pleased to see them. I remember thinking that they looked very healthy. The South African lifestyle and climate must suit them.

We drove the 15 miles back to their place in the Bezuidenhout (aka "Bez Valley") Valley, one of the suburbs of Johannesburg. Their "colonial" style bungalow was smallish in size with one bedroom, living room, bathroom and kitchen. "The Little House" was in the back garden area of "The Big House". The Little House had a little veranda with chairs on it, just like in the movies. I'm guessing it might have been the housemaid's, or servant's, house at some point in the past. Bez Valley looked just like the colonial style bungalow suburb built on a Roman road grid pattern I was expecting to see and it could easily have been lifted and dropped into a town in, say, Australia or New Zealand. You would be hard pressed to spot the difference.

Jenny had prepared an amazing, very welcome, meal consisting of "T bone steaks, big black things full of yellow stuff that were delicious, long green things like carrots, sweet things like potatoes, red wine and coffee". That's what I wrote at the time in my diary because I didn't like to ask what the vegetables were.

Then, after the meal, we went to see their "Big House" neighbours for a chat. The people who lived there were planning to sell up and move out apparently. So, Jenny and David said they were thinking of buying that and "The Little House" as well, which I thought was a good idea (they did buy both eventually).

7

After returning to The Little House, Jenny and David seemed to be more tired than me, but I guess I was probably running on adrenalin. So, they showed me how and where I would be sleeping and I "clicked" that they were hinting that it was bedtime, even though, to me, it was very early at only 9pm. I was to sleep in a bed that was going to be brought out every night into the living room. It turned out that it was quite comfortable. So, it was off to bed. I was a midnighter-2am type of person then, and still am, but not so good on the mornings.

The Tiny Black Dog

The next morning on the 9th, Jenny and David were up bright and early and left to go to work at 7:45am. She worked in a firm in the city and he worked at one of the universities. I took a photo whilst have a stroll around the suburb, and, as you can see the streets were wide, tree lined and with similar bungalow style properties on either side:-

Bez Valley

So, I was alone in The Little House and I thought I would take the opportunity to have an extra bit of a "sleep in", but I just couldn't. I was too excited. So, I gave up by 8:15am and was about to go out for a walk up to the shop on the corner for some bread, when I heard a tapping on the door. It was a lovely tiny black dog like nothing I'd seen before. It was about the size of a Yorkie, but looked like a pedigree Alsatian puppy. It was friendly and I learnt later, apparently popped in almost every day. I wonder what it was called?

Shaka The Cat

I also took the opportunity to start making friends with their cat Shaka (which they pronounced Charka). They'd named him after a fierce Zulu King and he seemed to possess many of the characteristics I imagine a Zulu King would have had too. He was quite a character and had clearly been in many battles and had the scars to prove it. He had only one eye, ragged claw ripped ears, a once broken rib and half his tail was missing. Like the real King Shaka, he had several wives in the pussy cat arena with whom he had an active life. He was dark grey in colour and was wary of anyone, like me, who was new, till he got to know you that was. As my stay wore on, he must have decided I was "ok" and became quite attached to me. The dog and Shaka just ignored each other though and seemed to co-exist quite happily in the same space.

"Only blacks eat brown bread".

Bit of a strange quote isn't it, "Only blacks eat brown bread"? So, you'll be wondering "what am I talking about?" Well, my first exposure to racial stereotyping was not what I expected. After meeting the little black dog and saying "hi" to Shaka, I went to the shop on the corner to get some bread. It was run by a Chinese man called Hoong. I asked for a loaf of brown bread and he looked very surprised, as if I had asked for chips, egg, beans and HP sauce in a Michelin 5 Star restaurant, and I couldn't understand why. He didn't explain his reaction to me at the time, but just served me and off I went, perplexed, with my brown bread back to The Little House. It bothered me all day, so I told Jenny and David about it later and they said "Ah, only blacks eat brown bread". But it was nice, so I decided I would continue to eat it too. Jenny and David also said they ate brown bread. They just ignored the convention.

"Whites", "Blacks", "Afrikaners", and "Cape Coloured"

By the way, I'm guessing some of you might be objecting to my use of the word "blacks", so I'd better explain. When I use the word "blacks" to describe people who are, well, coloured black, don't take that as a derogatory, or racist, term. It was normal vernacular in 1979 to refer to people by the colour of their skin where context warranted that. So, use of words to classify people such as "Whites", "Blacks", "Boers", "Afrikaners", "Indians", "Chinese" and "Cape Coloured" (mixed race) in South Africa and elsewhere were normal. I have used those here as a way of defining racial background in the context of 1979. I would argue that that is important when you are telling a story within the context of South Africa's apartheid regime which existed at the time. It will hopefully convey a sense of the tone in language that existed then. When I write this story in 2021-

9

22, labelling conventions of "Of Colour" or "BAME", etc, were unknown at the time. I have tried avoided using the word "Kaffir" though unless in absolute context, which some mainly Afrikaner Boer white people tended to use to refer to all blacks just as naturally they would if they were taking about coffee or marmalade. At the time it was already regarded in the UK as a politically incorrect and insulting term. So, some Boers I met used the term just as easily as my grandparents might have used "spastic" or "cripple" to describe people with cerebral palsy that we might classify "physically disabled" now. Who knows, by 2050, perhaps the term "physically disabled" will be seen as insulting too.

First Exposure to Extreme Poverty

My other introduction to the inequalities of the country was on the same walk to the shop to get the bread. It was almost out of a "real" Charles Dickens Novel. The shop was on the corner of the block and over the other side of the road there were three black men and two black women sitting around a fire they'd made on the grass verge. They looked very destitute and unhealthy too. I felt sorry for them because I had never seen anyone who was so obviously that poor before. As I say, it was like something out of one of Charles Dickens novels. Extreme poverty in the presence of middle class and immense wealth in an unjust socially stratified Victorian society. Not even the unemployed miners and their families in my home village in England, when the main local employee, a coal mine, closed in the late 1950s seemed to have been that poor. I remember being with my Granddad when he met up with massed groups of unemployed ex-miners in their flat caps and 3-piece suits, gathering on street corners just to chat and pass the time of day. But they never seemed that destitute. Thank goodness for the safety net of the Welfare State in the UK I thought. Not perfect, but at least you could only fall so far, whereas in South Africa it seemed that you could fall very far indeed.

How to "Google" in 1979

After arriving back at The Little House, I had my breakfast and after playing with the dog and persevering with the process of befriending Shaka, I went on the bus into the centre of the city. Remember 1979 was the time before PCs, laptops, modems, broadband, Wi-Fi, mobile phones, or the internet. There was no instant access to information like there was in 2021. So, I had to physically do my own searches in person via the tourist information office in the city to pick up brochures, free maps and so on and talk to the staff, as well as seek ideas from Jenny, David and their friends. That was so I could begin to form some more precise ideas on where and when to go on my big adventures, to add more colour to the pencil sketch of a plan I had in my head. Then, suitably weighed down with much brochure-wear, free maps and a mind buzzing with ideas, I met Jenny at her office later in the morning. It was a plush place with modern furniture etc. David arrived and we all went to the Wimpy Bar for lunch. That was very similar to the Wimpy Bars that existed in the UK at that time.

Who needs a Compass?

This is the actual map I picked up from Tourist Information in Johannesburg:-

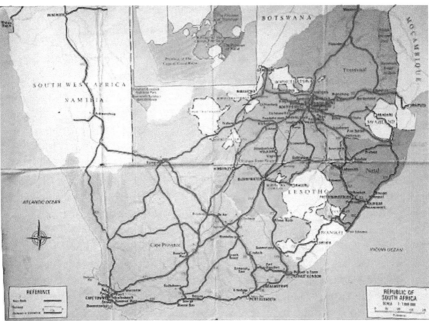

Map used to navigate around Southern Africa

Yes, I really did use that as my map to navigate my way around southern Africa. And I kept it safe as a little memento in a box for over 40 years. It was, to say the least, "strategic" and it didn't include Zimbabwe-Rhodesia as it was known then! I had to pick up another free map for that at the travel agent near the border in Musina. More on that later.

80p for a Wimpy Bar Meal

It was in the Wimpy Bar when I first realised how cheap it was in South Africa. I had a beef burger, with cheese, egg, tomatoes, chips and a milk shake for R1.20. At R1.85 to £1 that cost me about 80p. The service was excellent too. The waiter was polite and helpful and surprised me too because he called me "Sir". I think that was the first time outside of the British Army where I had been called "Sir" in an everyday place like a Wimpy Bar. Not at all like our Wimpy Bar staff in the UK where you would be lucky if they gave you the briefest of smiles, or even looked at you when you requested service, or wanted to place an order. That's when I noticed that all the staff working in the Wimpy Bar as waiters and waitresses were not white and that that was typical across many similar places I went to across the country. That was the other element in the cost-of-living equation. Jenny and David said that the Wimpy staff probably only earned R5 per day. So, in 1979 South Africa average "white" earnings were about R7,860 per year apparently and Blacks were R1,885 per year. That goes some way to suggest why the cost of food in the Wimpy Bar was so cheap. Exchange rates were also skewed in my favour, because of the effects of sanctions on South Africa due to their apartheid policies. Sanctions made the Rand less attractive on international currency markets.

His Own Office!

After lunch Jenny had to go back to work and I went back to the university with David who was a lecturer there. He showed me his office which he had all to himself. Very impressive! At the aerospace company where I had worked on my placement, only very senior managers had the privilege and status of having their own office. He even had his own name plaque on the door. I remember thinking "How cool is that!!". He introduced me to other people he worked with in the department and all of them were very friendly and made me feel most welcome. Then I left him to his work and went to explore the university campus, especially the impressive classical Greek temple style façade of the Great Hall. I only got as far as the café though, because one of his friends that I had just been introduced to had migrated there with some others. He insisted I came and sat with them and we talked for over 2 hours about South Africa, Zimbabwe-Rhodesia and the UK. .

"Let's have a drink with The PiG"

It wasn't long before 5pm came and I made way back to David's office and he said, "Let's have a drink with the PiG". Obviously, I had no idea what the PiG was, but he explained it was the Post Graduate Club. The words "Let's have a drink with "The PiG" though were rather perplexing until I went inside and all became clearer, because there was a stuffed boars head on the wall wearing sunglasses and a university neck tie.

Jenny arrived a little later and we had a really good time, ably assisted by ample quantities of lager. There were quite a few characters there and they were all equally as friendly as the ones I had met earlier in the cafe. I noted in my diary that "several had beards, pot bellies, deep voices and told dirty jokes".

Revolving Panoramic Superb Staff Restaurant

Jenny and David said we could all go on from there to the University Staff Restaurant for a meal. I was expecting a typical university canteen, but this one was, well, exceptional, except the word "exceptional" doesn't feel hyperbolic enough to describe what it was like. It was frankly amazing. The Staff Restaurant was a grand theatrical double-volume revolving restaurant on top of a 21-storey skyscraper called "University Corner" (formerly the Lawson Building). It was located on the corner of Jorissen and Bertha Streets and was pretty "new" then, having just been built in 1968. It really was an unbelievable incredible place with red velvet ruched curtains and a full 360 degrees view of the city from the restaurant, which slowly revolved around as you sat there. My only previous "comparable" place in terms of function, not appearance, was the canteen at the Management School in England, whose sullen staff served up "chips, beans with something fried, sausage roll or a pie" to students and lecturers alike. The South African equivalent was luxurious with modern furniture, carpets, a bar and we were served by waiters (all were not white again note) who were incredibly attentive and would do anything to help. We just sat there and they brought us everything we needed with incredible efficiency. I pushed the boat out, encouraged by my hosts, and treated myself to sirloin steak with all the trimmings. We all had the most expensive wine on the list. It cost me only R3, which was about £1.75 then, equivalent to around £7.50 in 2020. That was fantastic value which was made even better by the superb revolving panoramic views of the city lights that grew increasingly brighter as the sun set and night fell. It was marvellous. The only two comparable places I have been to in the UK since in terms of ambience and service levels was, firstly, the Grosvenor Hotel at an Annual Company Dinner and secondly, the revolving Tower Restaurant in Liverpool where I took my now wife to propose marriage to her over a very expensive meal (although when I checked in 2021 the Tower Restaurant had turned into Liverpool's Radio City studio).

Early to Bed

We left the restaurant by 9pm. Jenny and David were ready to go to bed by then. That was something I realised I would just have to get used to because, as I said, in the UK, I generally stayed up until at least midnight, and even a late as 2am, when I often had to tell myself to go to bed, even though my head frequently told me I didn't need to. Apparently, most people in South Africa went to bed at around 9pm, which surprised me. I wondered if it was because there was only one South African Broadcasting Corporation (SABC) TV channel. The content choice was less compared to that in the UK at the time. Plus, most people seemed to start work an hour or so earlier than in England. That was probably why.

"Top of Africa"

The next morning on the 10th July, Jenny and David were up and out again very early to go to work by 7.45am. They left me to sleep in, which was nice of them. When I got up, I spent the early morning writing letters home. I also wrote in my diary:-

> *"It's now Tuesday 10th July I have been here for 3 days. I've seen so much since I arrived, I'm having trouble putting it all in order so that it will make sense. I think the best thing I can do start at the beginning. I'm drinking some tea now as I write this. I have this dubious theory that's because Johannesburg was about 6,000 feet above sea level the water boils quicker than ours and that is why the tea is so bloody awful. It does, yes, but perhaps the water "contents" could be the cause too? Still never mind, I suppose it will have to do. Maybe South African tea plants are rubbish. Anyway, enough of that."*

After that I headed off on the bus into the city again to have lunch with Jenny and David. They took me to the fabulous University Staff Restaurant again. I couldn't wait. I decided to have steak again. Afterwards they returned to work and I continued my walking exploration of the city.

Do you get that tingling feeling, together with a rather worrying feeling that you might jump off, when you go up to the top of incredibly high buildings and look down at the ground far below? Well, I do. I just had to go up to the top of the tallest building in Africa at the time. It was the Carlton Centre , a 223 metre, 732 feet, 50 story skyscraper and shopping centre located in downtown Johannesburg.

By 2021, apparently, it has been relegated to be the 2nd tallest building in Africa. As you can imagine the view from the 50th top floor, known as the "Top of Africa", aka "Carlton Panorama", was impressive. The tingling sensation in my hands when looking down was there in abundance and caused me to take three steps backwards from the edge. The sky was blue, so I could see for miles in all directions. I had a couple of coffees in the

Wimpy Bar too when I had finished my tour to "recover". One thing worth commenting on is that the winter weather at the time was like summer in the UK, drier, much drier, sunny yes, with barely any clouds, except it was their winter. To me it was warm enough to wander around as if I was in the UK in summer in my shirt sleeves, but to the locals, it was cold. I must have stuck out like a sore tourist thumb.

"Whoops, I'm not black!"

I continued to explore the sights of Johannesburg on the 11th and 12th July. One of my most memorable experiences of apartheid was at the Railway Station. What I didn't realise was that there were different platform areas for "Whites" and "Blacks" and I innocently wandered into the "Blacks' only" zone. I only realised what I had done when I looked around and noticed everyone was staring at me with a puzzled look on their faces as if I was some kind of alien being. I realised with a dawning realisation that "they" were all not white and I was. In fact, I was the only white face there. I had the distinct feeling at that point I was somewhere I should not be. So, I calmly retraced my steps back to the entrance. It was there that I spotted the "Blacks Only" sign. I'd walked past it without noticing. I told Jenny and David about that later and they said they all probably thought I was a policeman, because they would be the only white people who would nonchalantly saunter like that into that part of the station. Ah, well, not many tourists will have had that experience, I guess. Of course, the sad thing about it all was that there was a system in place that segregated people based on skin colour.

Where I grew up in the far corner of NW England virtually everyone was white and many were working class and unemployed, except for doctors at the local hospitals. Many were from Africa or the India sub-continent. With hindsight you could look on my early exposure to people who were not white as a kind of "reverse colonialism". As in, in "the colonies" the doctors would have been more likely to be white and the population they served black, or coloured. After that I returned to The Little House and ended the day by catching up on some letter writing home.

3. HEADING EAST TO ST LUCIA

My Lucky Day

The following day, Friday the 13th, is viewed as unlucky for some, but for me, it was a lucky day. Jenny and David had kindly taken time off work so they could take me on holiday with them to Barberton in the De Kaap Valley fringed by the Makhonjwa Mountains of East Transvaal. Then we would be heading for Mbabane in the Kingdom of Swaziland (now renamed Eswatini) and then onto St Lucia in Natal (KwaZulu-Natal). That was the first of my big adventures. I'm using the place names as they were back in 1979, but as you can see, I'll try and note the 2022 names too if they have been changed after the end of the apartheid era.

We drove off in a VW minibus which they called "the Combie" for about 4.5 hours, 220 miles, to Barberton:-

Barberton Impala Hotel and Stock Exchange building

When we arrived in Barberton, we checked into the Impala Hotel and stayed for two nights. Here's our route:-

Johannesburg to St Lucia and back

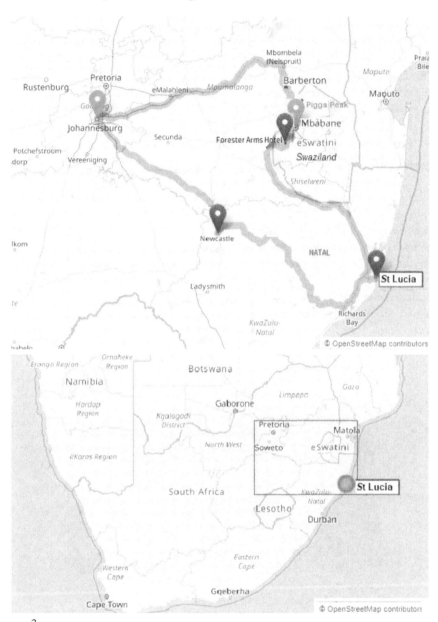

3

The Impala Hotel was excellent. In fact, one thing I quickly realised was that all the hospitality venues I went to had levels of service that far surpassed that which I had become accustomed to in the UK. I'd worked as a 2nd Chef in a Hotel two nights a week in the 6th form whilst I was at

17

school and latterly as a barman. So, I had some real "customer service benchmarking experience" to go off from both sides of the fence.

We went on a walkabout exploration of the town. The photo above on the right shows the outside of the De Kaap Exchange on Pilgrim Street. Barberton. It was built in 1887 and was only the second Stock Exchange in the Transvaal. Only its facade remains today, but thankfully, it had been designated as a national monument. So, it will more than likely continue to be preserved as part of the "Rainbow Nation's" heritage.

Eureka City, Gold Rush Ghost Town

The following day we drove out in the "Combie" to explore Eureka City, a gold rush ghost town in the hills about 4 miles from Barberton. The journey to it was an experience. The 5-mile rutted and pot holed dirt "road" leading up the pass to a height of about 1,500 feet had gradients that varied between 1:18 and a very challenging 1:6. Only vehicles with good ground clearance and sufficient power could use it. Fortunately, "the Combie" was one of those with raised axles for off road use and with use of low gears, and ample patience and adept driving by David, we made it to the top.

Eureka City was established in 1885 and was occupied until about 1895. It had three shops, three hotels, a bakery, chemist, racecourse, music hall and bars to cater for the 700, or so, gold diggers who lived there:-

Unknown author, Public domain, via Wikimedia Commons

It was completely abandoned once the retrievable gold had been extracted. It was a fascinating place and, as I gazed out over it, I wondered if it could be taken as an illustration of what the remains of human civilisation could look like 80 or so years after a devastating nuclear war. Nature had retrieved most of it by then. Its place on an inaccessible ridge, with limited water supplies, were probably its Achilles heel, and so it remained, with only the spectacular, breathtaking and beautiful mountain scenery to keep it company:-

The photo on the top left shows the Victoria Hotel ruins. The top right photo is of what was once the main street. The middle two photos show off the views from the ridge and the bottom two show Jenny and David walking through where the city used to be.

Afterwards, with equally skillful driving by David, we successfully negotiated the "helter skelter" ride back down the pass to arrive in one piece back at the hotel.

How to convert a Combie into a Masserati

On the 15th we checked out of the Impala Hotel and drove over the border into Swaziland, partly by way of a dirt road pass over the mountains in "the Combie". Unfortunately, excellent driving skills were no match for the terrain's revenge and a protruding rock next to an adjacent pothole eagerly ripped the rear section of the exhaust off as the rear wheel dropped into the hole. That was better than the engine sump being cracked open in the middle of nowhere. We would have had a long trek back to civilisation if we had broken that. After the incident, "the Combie" sounded like a real Masserati. If we wanted to sneak into Swaziland, there was no chance of that now. Along the way we enjoyed more breath-taking views looking down over the edge of the road:-

The road to Piggs Peak

Amazing Views

Jenny took my photo with the vast panorama spreading out to the distant horizon behind me on the edge of the ridge on the road leading to our next stop at Piggs Peak in Swaziland. Big mountains and big sky.

Me and the amazing views in Swaziland

Another strange sight (to me anyway) was where some Swazis chose to build their villages. This one, for example, was built into man-made terraces set along the steep sides of a mountain, apparently a long way from any source of obvious water. Was that an unhindered choice of theirs, or was it the only affordable land available for them?

A Swazi village clinging onto the mountain slope

Short Back and Sides Sir?

I also must mention the strangest hairdressers I had ever seen to that point, or since for that matter, on our way to Piggs Peak:-

Barbers shop on the way to Piggs Peak

The sign is difficult to read in the original photo on the left above, showing the spot where the local "hairdresser" had enterprisingly set up their "shop". The "blow up" of the photo on the right shows the sign more clearly, says:

"Thula …yo   Hair Dressing Saloon 50"

The 50 probably meant 50 cents. So, in the Swazi Lilangeni currency, one Lilangeni in 2021 was worth about 5p. So, a haircut cost probably about 2.5p. I had to admire the enterprise of the person who ran the "shop". They'd set it up with no overheads for the capital outlay of one painted tin lid, a concrete block "seat" and a dustbin for the cut hair, plus some scissors and perhaps a manual shaver. The young man selling newspapers looked like he was also equally enterprising too, albeit in a scarce market with what seemed to be only a little potential custom from passersby.

Piggs' Peak

We eventually arrived at our next destination of Piggs' Peak, a little town in the highlands of northern Swaziland. We stopped for a walkabout exploration before we continued on our way. In the top left photo below the main town store is on the left and the BP petrol station on the right. The busy market, top right below, shows several stores selling goods to locals from the many stalls:-

Piggs' Peak

I couldn't figure out whether the row, bottom left, above were shops, fast food cafes, takeaways, or something else such as bars or even basic accommodation, but the locals were hanging around outside and at the counters. The photo on the right, I am not sure of now, but it looks like an official building with a flag flying in the area in front and entrance barrier in the vertical position. A police station perhaps?

On to Mbabane, the Capital

After leaving Piggs Peak we headed down the main road to the capital city of Swaziland called Mbabane. The photo on the left below is the view as we approached. That's located astride the Mbabane and Polinjane rivers in the Mdzimba Mountains: -

Mbabane, capital of Swaziland

That evening we stayed at the Holiday Inn in Mbabane. The city is about as big as St Annes near Blackpool, but much less developed. To me it was less developed, with very modern buildings in the centre that contrasted with the poorer accommodation occupied by many Swazis in other areas. The hotel wasn't as good as the Impala Hotel we had just come from and I took my lead from Jenny and David who didn't feel it was safe to venture out on foot to explore the city that evening, so we didn't.

The Road to The Forester Arms Hotel

On the 16th July we checked out of the Holiday Inn and drove for about 12 miles SW of the capital Mbabane to stay at The Forester Arms Hotel.

Usutu Forest pulp and paper mill

On the way from we passed the Usutu Forest pulp and paper mill at Bhunya in the Mazini District of Swaziland. The owners, SAPPI, provided considerable support to the local economy from the wages of locals they employed apparently with significant "knock on" benefits for various supporting services and suppliers. They also owned over 135,000 acres of surrounding, mainly pine tree, forestry that fed the mill with its raw material. Looking the mill up again on the internet in 2021 showed that it was subsequently closed as uneconomical but restarted operations after it was sold by SAPPI to a Swazi company called Montigny Investments . We also saw forest fires (top left photo below) as we drove along. It was fascinating to see the many traditional Swazi homesteads built with mud straw walls and thatched roofs:-

I had the feeling that I might be observing scenes as if I had time travelled back in time in Jules Vern's time machine to a Britain where roundhouses were prevalent during the pre-Roman Bronze and Iron Age 2000 plus years ago. What really struck me was the contrast in living standards between the Swazi native villagers living in their traditional way in wattle and daub wall roundhouses with thatched roofs, with no obvious source of instant electricity, running water, or central heating, or flushing toilets and bathrooms, and "us". We were used to a complex life with our fully plumbed in and wired-up western houses. I wondered who was the happiest? Who had the best quality of life?

Swazi countryside and homesteads

I had the feeling that I might be observing scenes as if I had time travelled back in time in Jules Vern's time machine to a Britain where roundhouses were prevalent during the pre-Roman Bronze and Iron Age 2000 plus years ago. What really struck me was the contrast in living standards between the Swazi native villagers living in their traditional way in wattle and daub wall roundhouses with thatched roofs, with no obvious source of instant electricity, running water, or central heating, or flushing toilets and bathrooms, and "us". We were used to a complex life with our fully plumbed in and wired-up western houses. I wondered who was the happiest? Who had the best quality of life?

Back in Time

Passing more stunning scenery along the way, it didn't take long before we arrived at our next stop, the isolated and tranquil Forester Arms Hotel.

Swazi mountain scene

The hotel was set in about 1,500 acres of stunning mountain pine forest in the Mhlambanyati District of Swaziland. Its colonial ambiance made it feel like we were stepping back in time to the British Empire when Swaziland was a British Protectorate. Mind you, that wasn't long before we arrived. The kingdom only became fully independent in 1968:-

Forester Arms Hotel

On the 17th, the weather was beautiful and sunny, so we went for a walk in the forest by the hotel:-.

Country walk from the Forester Arms Hotel

After that we spent the day relaxing and sunbathing by the hotel pool where we had the surprising bonus of seeing a fashion parade practice for the real event the hotel had scheduled for a few days' time. All the beautiful models came down to do a trial run. So, there we were relaxing beside the hotel swimming pool with all the models gliding by. It was tough, but I just had to grin and bear it.

Marvellous to have you ... Super!

Another notable memory I recall from staying there was the manager (or perhaps it was the owner) and especially his accent, He said he was a retired army officer with what would have passed as a very posh Home Counties BBC English accent. The surprising thing though (to me) was that during our conversations he said he was a local who was born there and, when I asked him, he said his accent wasn't unusual for the white descendant of British settlers in Swaziland and Natal at that time. His daughter's accent was the same too. I'm not being negative or critical, as they were both very nice. They also frequently added the word "super" to the end of sentences. Such as "It's absolutely marvellous to have you here, super".   She was a very attractive and lovely person. Her personality and attitude were so infectiously positive. She might have been called Ruth, but I am not sure now. Memory fades with time. I imagine she went onto a successful career in something like hotel management, hospitality, marketing, advertising or PR. A lovely person.

In the evening, after a very nice dinner together, I have very fond memories of relaxing "in paradise", lounging on the colonial style veranda looking out at the incredible forest views, drinking several ice-cold lagers and chatting with the manager and his daughter. I remember feeling relaxed and very happy to be there.

Sublime Saint Lucia

On Wednesday the 18th we checked out of the hotel and set off on a long 230-mile, 6 hour, drive down the winding roads to the beautiful town of St Lucia on the Natal coast. When we arrived, we checked into the plushest hotel yet, called the Lakeside View Hotel . I'm not sure if it is still there, but it was very "British Empire" in style and reminded me very much of a British Army Officers' Mess. All the waiting on staff wore white mess uniforms with black dicky bow ties, black trousers with red stripes up the sides. To pick a phrase our previous host's daughter would have used, the service was "absolutely super". I wrote in my diary "there is no way I am going to enjoy an English hotel again with their second-rate service and their 'couldn't give damn waiters". The othe"r noticeable change was the climate on the coast. Even though it was officially winter, it was hot to me during the day. The area around the hotel was beautiful. Immediately in front of it was an inland lake that was said to be full of crocodiles and hippos, but I didn't see any. The crickets made a hell of a noise all night that I found strangely relaxing.

St Lucia itself was lovely. McKenzie Street was the main street where our hotel was located along with several others, shops, restaurants and bars. Other streets had been imaginatively named and included Flamingo St, Pelican St, Hornbill St, Kingfisher St and Sandpiper St. as well as Dolphin Avn and Beach Rd, St Lucia felt like it was located on an island because we had to drive over a causeway bridge over the "lake" or inland estuary to access it.

Excellent Shark Fishing in the Surf

On the 19th July I spent most of the day sun bathing and relaxing as well as going for a walk around the St Lucia and to see the Indian Ocean which was only five minutes' walk away:-

Indian Ocean

I had a dip in the sea, as in, a paddle, just so I could tick off the Indian Ocean as yet another ocean I had been in. I restricted my paddling to the shallows instead of swimming, having read the subtle warning "hint" in the hotel's brochure about the shark fishing,

*"Guests can enjoy excellent shark fishing in the surf
just off shore".*

As in, they might just snack on any unsuspecting tourist who foolishly ventured out too far. So, I didn't fancy my chances having read "Jaws". I wish I could have gone swimming though, because the water was warm and the waves would have gone right over my head. I had one strange experience though. I was standing on the edge of where the waves were washing up the beach and when a rogue one came in so fast that, from standing on dry sand to being up to the waist in water, took about a couple of seconds. I did wonder if I had just experienced a mini tsunami tidal wave, perhaps caused by some minor seismic activity offshore. I would have had a great time on a surfboard too. Still, I decided I presented far too tasty a meal for any hungry sharks out there to take that risk (although the risks I took later in the holiday were much greater in comparison).

Weekend Petrol Ban

On Friday the 20th, after staying at the hotel for two nights, we had to make our way back to Johannesburg. International sanctions against the South African government's apartheid policy had resulted in a need to ration petrol. The Organization of Petroleum Exporting Countries (OPEC) members proclaimed an embargo against selling oil to South Africa in 1977. So, as Jenny and David said the government had introduced a weekend petrol ban and, as they were back into work on Monday, they had no choice but to set off on the long drive back and go back on Friday.

My First Safari

On the way back we had a drive through a game reserve. That was my very first safari, so it was exciting. It was a bit like a super-sized Longleat without the safety fences. I'm not sure which one it was looking back, but looking at a modern map it could have been either the Hluhluwe– iMfolozi Park, Thanda Reserve or Manyoni Reserve, which all seem to be close to the road we were travelling back along. We passed a man along the way dressed in the traditional attire of a Zulu whose job seemed to be to entice passers by into the Safari Lodge. He kindly agreed to have his photo taken:-

Traditional Zulu Attire at the Safari Lodge

I shot the lot

In those days there were no digital cameras, or mobile phones with cameras, where you could take almost as many photos and videos as you liked and storage space allowed, with no additional cost. That is except the small amount of power consumed and if you decided to buy, or print, paper ones. Back then, 35mm colour film came in pre-packed cassettes typically containing sufficient film to take 24 or 36 photos. You could have either slides, or prints, developed from the negatives. So, in 1979 a 24-exposure film cost about £1.50 and a 36, £2. On top of that it cost another £1 or so to get the film processed into slides or prints. So that's £2.50 to £3 per film. In 2020 that is equivalent to £12.50 for 24 and £15.50 for 36 exposures. So, film was not cheap, especially for a young student like me. During our drive through the game reserve, we saw lots of wild animals, including monkeys, baboons, pigs, deer, and zebras, but no leopards, rhinos, or lions. Just as I shot off my last film, we rounded the corner and a whole troupe of baboons crossed the road.

Looking back, I could tell I was excited on the safari because I shot every animal that popped up [with my camera fortunately] as we drove along the dirt roads that wound through the bush, most of which turned out to be slightly out of focus:-

Natal safari snapshots

How to skin a crocodile

The crocodiles and hippos must has known I was coming too as we didn't see any of those either. Until that is, we visited a crocodile farm on the way back and I had reloaded the camera with a new film. There were some quite big, magnificent crocodile "specimens" there. I felt it was a great pity that they were in captivity and that they were destined to end up as exotic meat, luxury handbags, belts, shoes, purses and wallets at some point.

Crocodile Farm

On the other hand, did that enhance the chances of the ones living in the wild to stay alive? At the farm they were just like pigs, sheep and cows were they not?

That's Cheap Boss

After we had been to the farm, we set off on our way again until we came upon one of those stalls the locals set up by the side of the road to sell goods, souvenirs and food produce they make on their Kraals to earn some hard currency: -

Typical roadside stall selling local produce

They could presumably then use that cash to buy other goods and services. Jenny saw some straw carpets with fancy patterns that she quite liked. So, we parked up to browse the stalls. While she was haggling over the carpets' price, a young boy, about age 10 at a guess came up to me with a carved wooden bird and a crocodile he said he had made. He was an impressive "salesman" for someone so young. I imagine he went on in later life to a hopefully successful career as a businessman in post-apartheid South Africa. I'll try and get the accent right, not because I am making fun of him, he was special, but because I want to convey the conversation in his accent:

"Heey Boss, you wanna buy di croc, it's vaaarrry cheap, only 2 Rant?".

So, I said "No I'm not interested, but thank you anyway".

Jenny had prepped me to say that and then look the other way. That's the way to negotiate the price apparently. Then he said :

"I'm vary vaaarrry hungeeery Boss I need da money to getta some food Boss, Eh Boss,… what do yoouu say…. 1.50 Rant eh? That's cheap Boss!".

By that time though Jenny had bought her carpets and she was keen to go. Just then two other young boys came running up with a crocodile and a bird carving. One of them immediately offered me his for only 50 cents. The first boys face dropped, so I offered R3, plus the extra cents in loose change in my pocket. I was impressed by their effort. So, I ended up the proud owner of all three boys' carvings. That's not much, about £1.75, but they were clearly happy and Jenny said that they might only earn about R5 per day working in "proper jobs". So R3 was a lot to those boys. I wondered how they survived on such low incomes, but imagined there were probably two economies in operation, with perhaps much lower prices and less need to buy things with cash. The wage differentials, cost of meals in restaurants, and the price of a road side haircut in Swaziland, had given me the first clues to that economic differential.

The drive back to Jo'burg was long. We ended up driving by Newcastle, and on and on, for around 8 hours in addition to the 4 hours we spent touring the game reserve, croc farm and stall browsing. So, it was after 10pm when we arrived back. That was well past their 9pm bedtime, so everyone went straight to bed and the bags were left in the car until morning.

Living on the Ridge

The next day, Saturday 21st July, was a day for relaxing and reading letters from home that were waiting for me on return. Then I went to explore the hills that formed the ridges of Bez Valley. I had great views from the top towards the city centre of Johannesburg and across the valley:-

Views of Johannesburg from the ridge above Bez Valley

The natural vegetation up on the ridges looked like the kind you would expect to find in semi-arid eco-systems with cactus like plant, dry grasses and the like. It was easy to imagine up there on the ridges what the place might have been like before the gold rush brought the city into being.

Squash with Altitude

On Sunday 22nd, David and I went to the university in the afternoon to play squash. He beat me twice and I won once, but he played every week and he was more used to the environment. He explained that I was breathless because Jo'burg was about 6,000 feet above sea level so the air was thinner. The squash really tired me out; the sweat was literally dripping off me. I wrote in my diary to myself "Mind you a few more sessions like that I should do better".

Totally Wasted

One of the blokes we were playing squash with invited us round to his place for a few drinks in the evening. Everyone drank a bit too much, I think. I know I did. His hand kept "slipping" when he was pouring my whiskey. I must have had about 6 double, or triple, whiskeys. Thing was though, I felt fine until the time came to leave, and I stood up, I nearly keeled over. I thought to myself at the time that nobody noticed that I was having great difficulty walking in a straight line. Of course, they did. It was more like two forward, one back, and a quick step to the right, then one to the left. Totally wasted. Anyway, I managed to pour myself into the car . When we arrived back, I drank as much water as I could to dilute the alcohol in the hope that it would reduce the hangover. Then I crashed out asleep, literally, as my head hit the pillow.

Catch Up Time

On Monday 23rd I woke up feeling rough, as a stiff as a crutch and with a cracking hangover. So, I drank lots more water, milk and coffee to clean my system out and had a walk up the street for some fresh air. However, I quickly realised I had also picked up a stomach bug and spent quite a bit of time running to the toilet because of it. So, I didn't venture far from The Little House and spent time catching up on my writing and reading letters home. I tried to eat some baked beans but couldn't manage more than a couple of mouths full. Also, I noted that I had not had a cigarette for three days now and didn't feel like one either. It wasn't playing squash; it was the drinking, or perhaps the local water. No surprise there then. I spent much of that week sitting on the veranda sun bathing and reading Henri Carriere's great book: "Papillon" as well as dealing with the consequences of my stomach bug. I eventually finished the book and writing and couldn't think of anything else to do. I'd explored Jo'burg by now. Besides I didn't come to South Africa to read books, or be ill. On Sunday the 29th I went into the city again to play squash. I was feeling much better. I didn't record who won that time. Wonder why? After that I went round to see Pauline at her house. She was a "Technical Assistant! I'd met at the university and she had invited me round for the afternoon and evening. She had prepared me a meal and we drank rather a lot. I had a long chat to her about my plans for adventure and my desire to explore the whole country. By the time I was leaving, at the end of the day, I decided it was time to put those plans into to immediate action. Besides, there's a saying that house guests are like fish. After three days both can go off a bit. I'd been there for more than that by then and I sensed I owed Jenny and David a little respite from my presence in their small one-bedroom house. So, on my return I discussed my plans with them. I could see they were rather concerned that I was going to hitch hike my way around in line with my limited budget. I promised I would be very careful and, so, with some trepidation they wished me luck and said to come back to their place on my return.

4. LET THE HIKING BEGIN

"Are there any Good Buddies out there?"

So, on Monday 30th July at 9:30am one of their retired friends called Arthur, (married to Iris) popped round and he kindly drove me to the outskirts of the city. I started hitch hiking to Cape Town:-

First leg of the hitch hiking …to Port Elizabeth

You might be wondering why the map shows a route leading only to Port Elizabeth (now renamed to Gqeberha) and not to Cape Town. More on why that happened later, but basically, when you are hitch hiking, you are only partially in charge of your own destiny. It took me two hours to get my first lift from a man called John who had a CB radio. Frequently during the lift, he went on the air to say, "Are there any Good Buddies out there who can give a buddy a lift to Cape Town?". Pity there weren't any, but it was quite fascinating.

Contribution to Global Warming

He dropped me off at his destination where he worked near a massive industrial complex spewing huge amounts of pollution into the atmosphere. I think it was probably the Sasol refinery that made oil products from coal at a place near the town of it was named after, Sasolburg, about 55 miles south of Jo'burg. Here's a couple of photos I took through the haze:-

Sasol refinery

At the time South Africa was subject to international trade sanctions, including oil, in protest against their apartheid policy. They had ample coal supplies from mines they operated, so were able to make substitute oil and petroleum products from it using methods developed in Germany as well as use the fuel to generate electricity. That alleviated some of the energy pressure from sanctions. How many billions of tons of carbon has that contributed? Of course, back then, the words "global warming" were not part of people's normal vocabulary It had only just started to penetrate the scientific community. The first scientific paper had only just been published in 1975. So, the problem didn't register with the overwhelming majority of people, including me. `-

Paratrooper to Bloemfontein

After that I had no problem with lifts, a farmer's son, then two tough Afrikaners, who kindly bought me lunch and then 3 army officers, who were very interesting and good to chat with about politics and the war going on in South West Africa (now Namibia). I made it as far as Bloemfontein by 5.30pm just as it was getting dark. The main highway by-passed the city but they said my best chance of getting a room for the night was in the centre, so they dropped me off at the turn off before they headed off west to their base. It didn't take long before I managed to get a lift into the centre with a paratrooper officer called Max, age about 25 or so, who was going on leave. He drove me to the Orange Hotel. It was a good, if basic, hotel. He stayed for a few beers and was great fun, then he used the payphone in the lobby to call his girlfriend to let her know he was back in town. He came over to say he was going to meet her, but he'd be back shortly with her and her best friend and we would all go out together for a great night out. But they didn't return. Guess he was "waylaid" after many weeks away from his girlfriend's charms. So, disappointed, I washed some clothes in the sink and hung them up to dry, had a shower and went to bed.

It would be worth explaining that I was travelling very light with a set of clothes in my rucksack, toothbrush etc, camera, rolls of film, notebook to record my journey, diary, passport, plus the set of clothes on my back that I wore each day and just the shoes on my feet. I washed the set of clothes that I've been wearing that day in the hotel bedroom sink, or bath, as required and hung them up on hotel coat hangers overnight to dry off. That routine worked very well. If I ran short of anything, I knew there should always a shop somewhere, or other…eventually. That always springs to mind when I see how much luggage most people pack to go on holiday.

"It will be lekker!".

The next morning, the 31ˢᵗ July, I arose early and went to the restaurant of the hotel for breakfast as soon as possible and then checked out to re commence my journey. I quickly realised that a city centre is probably the worst place to be to try to hitch hike. I had to walk 9 miles out of the city before I managed to get into a position where I could pitch effectively for my first lift. I did "stick my thumb out" along the route, but no one stopped. It was a nice blue sky, sunny day, and in the morning, it was fresh and cool. So, I welcomed the opportunity for a bit of exercise. The first lift I managed to get took me a few miles out of the city into the open countryside, but not very far along the highway towards Cape Town. It was still welcome. I was luckier with the next one though, because a very pretty girl pulled up called Ann. She said she was going all the way to Port Elizabeth on the coast (that has since been renamed "Gqeberha"). Port Elizabeth wasn't exactly on a direct route to Cape Town, but I thought "why not". So, I accepted the lift and off we went. She took the slightly more western route heading via the small town of Colesburg through the Highveld area on the edges of the Great Karoo Desert. As can be seen from the photo I took below the vegetation was sparse and of the type you would expect to find in such a semi-arid area.

Ann and I got on very well. The conversation flowed easily, and we were enjoying each other's company very much. She said she was 20 and studying in Johannesburg and was on her way to Port Elizabeth to see some family and friends. I'm not sure exactly where it was along our journey, but at one point we were driving along a straight stretch of road almost from horizon to horizon through the Highvelt. It was still a bright sunny, blue sky, day. We'd stopped at the side of the road for a while for a short rest break from driving and to stretch our legs. We couldn't see any other vehicles ahead, or behind us. The reason I mention this is because of the memorable experience of being in a vast place where no other human habitation, or presence, or noise, was evident, other than the road of course. The sheer emptiness of the place was marvellous, and the silence was complete apart from the soft synchronised sound of what were probably crickets and other insects chirping away in the scrub. There were several kinds of semi-desert plants dotted around and a little way off about a mile, or so, to the right of the road, there was a hill approximately 300-400 feet high. So, Ann said,

"Come on, let's climb that hill. The views from the
top will be lekker!!"

I asked what "lekker" was and she said it's just Afrikaans for something that was going to be great, fantastic. So, after briefly thinking this girl is so impulsive, but great fun, I agreed, and we set off through the bush on our

39

little adventure and climbed to the top of the hill. My favourite pass time back in England was walking the mountains of the Cumberland Lake District anyway ("fell walking"). We both sat there taking in the full 360 panorama to every horizon. It was so beautiful. There still weren't any other vehicles on the road, other than ours, in either direction as far as we could see. It was totally quiet. We stayed there for quite a while enjoying each other's company and the view. It was quite surreal. When I'd set off from Bloemfontein that morning, I would never have predicted that at this point in the day I would be doing what I was doing right then.

I couldn't leave the summit of our little hill without taking photos from the top across the Highveld down to the road where we parked. That's the thin line running at a slight downward angle from roughly the middle of the photo to just above the right-hand corner. Ann's car is highlighted by the red circle below and "blown up" on the middle shot and, more so, on the right. The photos were taken from the top of the hill look,:-

Highveld hill top on route to Port Elizabeth

The view looking the other way from the top of the hill, shown left below, was also spectacular. On the walk down we came across as a huge insect. I'm not sure what it was, but it looked like a large cricket, or perhaps a locust type insect. I still haven't been able to identify it:-

Mystery Highveld insect

After ambling down the hill and back to the car we set off again, but our little expedition up the hill meant that we only made it to Cradock in the Eastern Cape, well after the sun had set.

What? Sleep in the back of the car?

Cradock was just over 250 miles from Bloemfontein and 150 from Port Elizabeth and sat on the Great Fish River (Groot Visrivier in Afrikaans). Ann was too tired and couldn't drive anymore and needed a rest she said. So rather than check into a hotel she thought we would be ok to just park up for a while. We pulled over in what we thought was a quiet place outside of town in the countryside about 100 yards, or so, up a sidetrack into the bush. Ann had an estate car which was big enough in the back to catch some sleep in, so we both tumbled into the rear of the car. It was summer in the UK, but of course it was mid-winter in South Africa. So, with no cloud in the sky, it became a cold winter night quite quickly and the temperature in the car dropped rapidly to very cold. So, to keep warm we felt it would be better if we just cuddled up to try and keep warm. I wasn't complaining. Let's just say that we managed to generate sufficient heat to compensate for the low temperatures.

The only problem was that we had unknowingly pulled over into a lay-by not very far from the main railway line from Port Elizabeth into the interior through Cradock and the Drakensburg Mountain range. As a result, we were disturbed by very long freight trains rumbling past at the rate of roughly one every hour, or so, through the night. Because we were "in the middle of nowhere" you could hear the train when it was still a long way off as a low rumble that, for the first one, caused me to wonder "what is that noise. Was it a convoy of army tanks, or lorries, or a train heading our way?" Gradually the rumble increased in volume and the unmistakable addition of metal clicks and clacks, the occasional squeal of metal wheels on railway lines identified it as a train and added to the rumbling noise until it reached the nearest point of the line to us about a quarter of a mile way in the darkness. Then it began a slow declining rumble as it headed off down or up the tracks into the distance like some great lumbering mechanical snake.

Still, we managed to get a little fitful sleep until 5am or so (just before dawn). It was now the 1st August. It was quiet, so any sound travelled well in the cold pre-dawn air. We began to hear the distant sound of about half a dozen or so men speaking in an African native language. Given where we were, it was most likely Xhosa. Looking up we could just make out shadows of men walking towards us down the road from the direction we had driven along in the growing light of dawn. It didn't look like they had spotted us

41

yet as they were still a way off and, of course, they were very unlikely to be expecting to see a car parked where it was either. As we had no idea who they were, what they were doing, where they were going, or more importantly, what would happen if they found us, we very quickly decided it would be safer to drive off ASAP. So, a quick decamp into the front seats followed, the car started first time and we pulled back onto the main road and sped off east before they reached us and we headed down the road towards Port Elizabeth again. It was still cold, but at least with the car running we could put the heater on and warm up as we drove along. The sun came up as we were passing through the Drakensburg Mountains. We had a brief stop to stretch our legs again by the impressive Great Fish River:-

Great Fish River

After that we made our way along the main road into Port Elizabeth which runs west along the coast, so as you drive along, the city looms larger and larger on the horizon. Here is a photo I took from the road:-

Port Elizabeth looms ahead

We arrived in Port Elizabeth that morning and Ann took me to a nice hotel on the southern end of the sea front. I didn't note its name, but it was between the road and the sea. She wanted me to come with her when she went to see her friends later that day. So, after checking in, dropping my bag off and freshening up, we drove off and arrived about mid-day in northern part of Port Elizabeth to meet them. Their single storey bungalow reminded me a little of a Roman villa. It had an internal courtyard bordered on three sides by the U-shaped rear of the property. There were about a dozen of her friends there sitting around a braii (BBQ) set up in the centre of the courtyard.

Want some Dagga?

Some of them were passing around rolled up "cigarettes" containing something that was quite strong smelling. When I asked, they said it was called "dagga". I'd never heard of that, so I asked about it and they said it was made from the hemp like plant that grew plentifully around the local area. That's similar to, or in the same family, as cannabis, both in appearance and in its "doping" effect apparently. They said to me that its use in South Africa was very widespread and "traditional", including among the local community, who had always cultivated and smoked it. Lately, they said, it was becoming more popular among the younger generations. Those that were passing the dagga around were all pretty laid back and stoned.

There were a couple of guys who appeared to be uneasy and none too pleased that Ann had brought me there. I felt rather uncomfortable observing a hushed conversation between her and them out of ear shot. That was clearly about me as brief concerned glances were being made in my direction, while I pretended not to look that way. My "alert level" grew, and I began to feel rather uneasy and to be frank, a little unsafe. So, I sauntered over and interjected to ask Ann if it would be ok for me to head back to the hotel as I was feeling rather tired. That worked, she took the hint and drove me back. She told me that they had a suspicion I might be an undercover policeman and she had tried to alleviate their concerns, saying that it was extremely unlikely I would just have happened to be hitch hiking as she was passing, Besides, I was clearly English. I'm not sure I completely understood that logic properly. Perhaps she meant that most of the police were Afrikaners? Ann then dropped me at my hotel and promised to come back later that evening, which she did. So, we spent an enjoyable evening together having a nice meal in the hotel restaurant.

Impulsive Cove Swim

The next day Ann returned, and we spent the day wandering along the beach. The fascinating thing about her was that she was rather impulsive and as a result gave me yet another surreal experience. We went for a short drive along the coast to a favourite place of hers. It was a small deep-water cove set into the beach, with a fringe of rocks that formed little rocky outcrops shaped rather like a horse shoe. It looked like a great swimming place. Out of the blue, she just said, "Let's go swimming", in an excited "thrill seeking", impulsive way, and promptly ran over to the edge, stripped off to not a lot and launched herself off the rocks, plunging about 5 feet into the deep pool below. Closely followed by a rather amazed, but a "what the Hell, why not", me.

Although it was sunny the sea was not exactly warm given that it was winter. We had fun messing about in the water, but to be honest I was rather off put and wary of the infamous white sharks that I'd heard lurked offshore from my trip to St Lucia. Ann said we were perfectly safe in the cove and our frolicking all went off without my credentials being put in jeopardy by shark's teeth.

Victorian Legacy

After letting ourselves dry off a little, we went back to town and Ann took me on an exploratory walk around Port Elizabeth where we saw the sights, including the beautiful City Hall, Queen Victoria's statue and the famous Horse Memorial: The Horse Memorial paid homage to the many horses that had suffered, or died, in the Anglo-Boer, 1899-1902, and had an inscription that caught my eye. So, I wrote it down:-

"The greatness of a nation consists not so much in the number of its people or the extent of its territory as in the extent and justice of its compassion"

Good, yes? The bronze Memorial was unveiled by the Mayor of Port Elizabeth, Alexander Fettes on 11th February 1905. Joseph Whitehead was the designer, and it was cast in Surrey, England, at the Thames Dillon works apparently.

After that we went back to the hotel and after another final enjoyable evening with Ann, we parted company sadly knowing that in the morning I would be leaving for Cape Town and almost certainly I would never see her again. The whole experience was rather surreal to the extent that I had to metaphorically pinch myself and say:

"Did all that really happen?".

5. THE GARDEN ROUTE TO CAPE TOWN

"Hoe ver is dit tot Kaapstad?"

So, on the 2nd of August I rose early, had breakfast in the hotel dining room and then, after checking out, I walked out to the western edge of town to get into position to hitch lifts via the Garden Route to Cape Town 475 miles away:-

Garden Route via Riversdale to Cape Town

My first lift was with a tough, weather-beaten, middle-aged Afrikaner farmer called Andre in his pickup truck. So, it started off when he pulled up and I asked:- "How far is it to Cape Town?". That was my original plan for the day, to get to there. "Hey you're British ehhh, jump in". . Must have been my accent. He said that the Afrikaans (Dutch derivative) for that question was almost pronounced the same way even though the spelling was slightly different: "Hoe ver is dit tot Kaapstad?" he said, to bring the point home. I'd not fully realised just how similar Dutch and English were. He was driving back west to his farm. The memorable thing about that lift was that we discussed many things as well as language similarities, and I was also lucky to listen to an Afrikaner's political viewpoints.

An Afrikaner's politics

Looking back with hindsight the interesting thing was that this was the first time I had had a lift with an Afrikaner who was keen to "educate" me. We talked about a range of topics, including the Great Trek, the Boer Wars (1880-81 and 1899-1902) between the Dutch Afrikaner (also called Boers) and the British Empire, the Nationalist apartheid policy, culture, racism, race relations, and a possible vision of the future. I mainly asked the questions and listened. So, I will share that here with you as it was said, as I recall it without editing out the intended meaning. You'll notice that throughout the conversation he called black African's "kaffirs" quite naturally, which today, and even then, outside of Afrikaner South Africa, would be seen as politically unacceptable. However, it would be wrong to censor that as it adds an important context to the discourse. Here are my notes from the time:-

The Great Trek was a major event. The Afrikaners wanted to get away from the British in The Cape. So, his ancestors trekked out to set up their own country to live how they wanted. It was clear from what he said that The Great Trek was still of great significance to Afrikaners. There seemed to be a strong religious element to it as well. They were mainly Protestant Calvinists and they seemed to believe that their Trek, which had many trials and tribulations along the way, must have had God's full support..... So, God was on their side. He mentioned that I should go and see the Voortrekker Monument in Pretoria that commemorates that event in his ancestor's history. He was very proud of that. It was clearly very revered, like a shrine. Later in the holiday I made a point of going to see that. More on that later.

His ancestors fought the British in two Boer Wars to try and stop the tide of British expansion into their lands. It became virtually impossible to stop though because the pull of gold was too much after it was discovered in Witwatersrand area and diamonds around Kimberley. That's why the wars happened.

He said the Apartheid regime policy was supported by the Bible. The kaffirs and whites were fundamentally different. Staying apart was best. It preserved both their cultures. Each could lead their life in the way they wanted.

Also, he was very keen to point out that his ancestors had occupied and developed land that was previously largely sparsely unoccupied by kaffirs if at all, or they had bought it legally from tribal chiefs. So, they did not steal the land from anyone.

The roads and cities had been developed by the Afrikaners [and British]. If the whites were not there, the kaffirs would still be living in their traditional tribal way. Many still were. He pointed out the occasional kraals we passed, little settlements containing mud wall round huts with straw roofs. Each would have a kaffir chief or head man with a "chief hierarchy" leading up to their "King".

He feared for the future. The younger kaffirs in the townships would get drunk and think nothing of chopping each other up with machetes. If "they" ever got the upper hand and things turned nasty it could be very bloody. Their tribal system was hierarchical, so democracy was not "normal". They would tend to vote along tribal lines regardless.

He advised me to stay well out of the "Bantu" tribal areas for my own safety. He said that those had been set aside by the government for the kaffirs and were semi-independent territories. If you look at the map I used they are clearly marked out on that. They were unrecognised by the international community and were reabsorbed into South Africa in 1994. Those included the Transkei and Ciskei for the Xhosa tribe, Bophuthatswana for the Tswana tribe, Venda for the Venda tribe and KwaZulu for the Zulus.

He went on to say that Europeans tended to think that all South African Black people were the same. Their tribes could be as different in language, culture and identity as say Germans were from the Spanish, or the Russians from the Chinese. There could even be greater racial prejudice between members of the various tribes. Several had different languages, cultures and social norms. Imagine the French accepting a German President, or a Xhosa accepting a Zulu? They were not one homogenous group at all and interracial tension and animosity between different tribes was more pronounced than it appeared. It was the whites who maintained a sense of neutral calm, stability and law and order, he said.

He also mentioned that kaffirs generally have very different attitudes to a lot of things. His people are God fearing. They work hard, with ambition, to build up their farms and invest wealth from one generation to the next (the Protestant Work Ethic). Many kaffirs, on the other hand, are relatively lazy and too relaxed about work. He likened their tribal system to our Scottish Clans

Finally, he thought of himself as an African, as in, an Afrikaner, not as a European, or a Dutch person. His ancestors had arrived at the Cape about 3-400 years ago. He spoke Afrikaans as his first language as well as English and the local African language too. He wouldn't be going anywhere, no matter what happened in the future. He said many British descendants were recent, first, second or maybe third generation settlers. So, they might still have links back to Britain and go back if things kicked off. Africa was very much his home. He wasn't going anywhere and God help anybody who tried to dispossess him of his farm, or threaten his people or culture. I believed that last sentiment. The Afrikaner's track record during the Boer wars against the might of the British Empire bore testament to Boer resilence.

The Many Languages of South Africa

I looked up "languages of South Africa" on Wikipedia recently and the map I found shows dominant first language distribution. It suggests it is broadly in line with "tribal" identity. There are 35 languages in total of which 10 are "official", plus English, which is still the "common" language apparently:-

Dominant languages in South Africa:
- Afrikaans
- English
- Sepedi
- Sesotho
- Southern Ndebele
- Swazi
- Tsonga
- Tswana
- Venda
- Xhosa
- Zulu
- None dominant
- Areas of little or no population

Source: Wikipedia (public domain image).

With hindsight I have great respect for Presidents F. W. de Klerk and Nelson Mandella from 1989-90 onwards, who started the transition to "one man, one vote democracy". That could have gone down a very bloody and violently road, but Nelson Mandella's "Rainbow Nation" is surviving…. ok, with a few bumps, potholes and crashes along the road, but surviving.

Eventually he arrived at the turn off to his farm and I thanked him and started to hitch again. I'm glad I met him, a "real Boer" and that he shared his views with me, even if I couldn't reconcile many of them with my own world view. It's always good to listen to others' points of view, even if your own are fundamentally different. Later, during my adventures, I had equally fascinating lifts with three young black political activists travelling from Musina back to Jo'burg and, also, with an ex-smuggler Zulu businessman on his way back from Durban to Soweto near Jo'burg. More on those later. Here's a view I took by the side of the road waiting for my lift to Cape Town to turn up:-

On the road to Cape Town from Port Elizabeth

I tried to find the precise location recently, but so far, no luck. In the distance you can see what I think are the Drakensburg Mountain range. Big country. That picture perhaps conveys some of the scale of the place.

The Garden Route with Sabrina

My next lift was with Sabrina. What a lovely name. I noted it down. She was on her way to see some friends in Cape Town. Well, that's where I was heading, so off we went. She was in her early 20's I guess and lived in Port Elizabeth. Her black hair, eyes and dark complexion hinted at her ancestor's Portuguese origin, but she was living in South Africa now after leaving

Mozambique. That had been a Portuguese colony for over 400 years until 1975 and a bloody civil war started in 1977 and was still ongoing in 1979. Virtually all the whites of Portuguese origin had left very quickly for their own safety and survival she said.

It was a long way to Cape Town, (about 460 miles). The scale of the country is huge. I had an unconscious bad habit of judging distances based on a UK scale, so frequently misjudged distances by a wide margin. So, Sabrina and I had quite a long time that day to chat driving along through the beautiful Garden Route National Park. The scenery was beautiful with mountains to the right and the coast and ocean to the left. We passed the seaside holiday beauty spots of Knysna, George and Mossel Bay

With hindsight, I could have stopped to explore all three places for a day or two. The scenery from Jo'burg up to the coastal area was largely dry and arid, but here it was much greener and more beautiful. It wasn't until I returned to South Africa in 2017 on a guided tour that I had a chance to return and address that gap. That's the subject of another book by the way.

Sabrina drove on until the evening until a little road side village called Riversdale in the Western Cape (about 300 miles from Port Elizabeth). She said she would have to stop for the day in a little hotel there. "So, would I also check in or stay by the road and hitch?" The amount of through traffic was negligible and I had no idea whether there would be anywhere to stay overnight further up the road. The safest option was to stay. So, I did likewise and booked into the same hotel and stayed the night.

6. CAPE TOWN

£1.70 per night at the YMCA!!

On the 3rd August, after breakfast, Sabrina offered to give me another lift which was very kind of her. So, we set off for the last leg into Cape Town and arrived about midday. She dropped me off at the Young Man's Christian Association (YMCA) hostel. I had done a bit of research beforehand in Jo'burg and discovered that the YMCA had a reputation for being the lowest cost, "best value" place to stay for students, etc, in Cape Town. As I was on a budget, that was a key consideration for me. It cost only R3.15 [equivalent to about £1.70] per night for bed and breakfast. Taking inflation into account that's equivalent to about £8.80 in 2020. It was great value. There were two YHAs in Cape Town then, Cape Town YMCA and Louie Botha YMCA. So, I can't be 100% sure, but I think it was the Cape Town YMCA that I stayed at.

Julia and Pizza

Having dropped me off at the YMCA, Sabrina went off to meet her friends. I thanked her for the lift. It was much appreciated. After settling into my little room, I went out to explore the city. In the evening I took up an invite to go to see Julia and her boyfriend Geoff. I wrote in my diary that Julia was a friend of Jenny and David, so I had met her already in Jo'burg at one of the social gatherings. I have a note that she worked at Sotheby's in Jo'burg. I'd guess she was probably around aged 21-24. She lived in an apartment in the city centre of Jo'burg at Wanders View in Hillbrow. I'd mentioned I was heading to Cape Town, and she said she was likely to be there too at the same time on holiday seeing her boyfriend who lived there. So, she had asked me to get in touch when I arrived in Cape Town. I called the number and we arranged to meet at her boyfriend's place. That was on the southwest coastal side of the city centre with Table Mountain to the rear and great views over the sea, harbour, and city to the front. Very swish. After chatting for a while, we all went out together for a meal to an Italian restaurant. Julia's boyfriend kindly insisted on paying, I protested, but he assured me he would be happy to pay, so I didn't argue further. It was very kind of him.

Romantic Poetry

The next day, Saturday 4th, I went to explore the city on foot starting with the museum. For some reason I was quite taken with a romantic poem I saw in an old greetings card that was on display and wrote it out in my diary:-

"The dearest wish my heart can form

Beloved one for thee

Is that thou may'st enjoy the bliss

Thy love bestows on me."

Rhodes Memorial on Devil's Peak

I also walked up to see the impressive Rhodes Memorial that commemorates the life of Cecil Rhodes (1853–1902). It was built on Devil's Peak against the backdrop of Table Mountain. It looked dominantly out over the city and to the northeast. It is said that it shows the way to the road / railway from Cape Town to Cairo that Rhodes dreamed would one day become a reality with all the land in-between part of the British Empire. The monument was built using Cape granite quarried on Table Mountain and was completed and dedicated in 1912. Rhodes played a major role during the foundation of the British Empire in Africa and even had a two countries named after him: Northern Rhodesia (Zambia) and Southern Rhodesia (Zimbabwe), where his body is buried. He also became incredibly rich. Its massive staircase had 49 steps (one for each year of Rhodes's life) leading to a semi-circular terrace and a rectangular U-shaped monument formed of pillars that looked like a Greek Temple. That contained a bust of Rhodes . At each side of the staircase were eight bronze lions and at the foot of those there was a bronze statue of a horseman. The inscription read:

"To the spirit and life work of Cecil John Rhodes

who loved and served South Africa. "

Here's some photos I took at the time:

Rhodes Memorial

At that time, in 1979, being at that monument made me feel proud to be British. When I was born in the 1950s, the British Empire and Commonwealth was still largely intact. Most colonies became independent from the mid-1960s onwards. Rhodes had achieved so much in his relatively short life, and I could understand why that memorial had been built. Of course, now, as I write this, the whole concept of one nation colonising another is viewed entirely differently by many, and Rhodes can be seen by some as an imperialist invader and even a murderer. Whatever your viewpoint on Rhodes, one thing is rarely in dispute, he made a very big impact during his short life which still reverberates through history today and probably will continue to do so well into the future as many a Rhodes scholar may be aware. After making my way back, I explored more of the city. It has a lot of character and history spanning back 400 or more years. The impressive South African Parliament Building and the equally impressive City Hall, were both neo-classical buildings built in the classical "British Empire" style designed to convey "soft power":-

The Famous Pig and Whistle Pub

Then, in the evening, taking advice from others at the YMCA on great places to go for a night out, I went to the famous and popular Pig and Whistle Pub in Rondebosch, Cape Town. The pub was full of students and others mainly aged circa "18 to 30". I bumped into a guy from St Annes, another from Blackpool and two others from Wales while propping up the bar. It's a small world. After that I went to the cinema to see the newly released 1979 James Bond film "Moonraker", starring Roger Moore. I enjoyed it as usual. I think I have seen every James Bond movie to date.

On Sunday the 5th August I went down to see the Castle of Good Hope and the National Art Gallery. In the evening I was back again at the Pig and Whistle Pub for several more Castle beers and a meal.

The next day, Monday 6th August, had some significance from a financial perspective. My paid aerospace company holiday leave ended that day, and my unpaid special leave began (as in no more pay). I went down to Muizemburg on the train, a little beach side town to the south of Cape Town. I took a walk along the sea front and spent a while on the beach before returning to the YMCA.

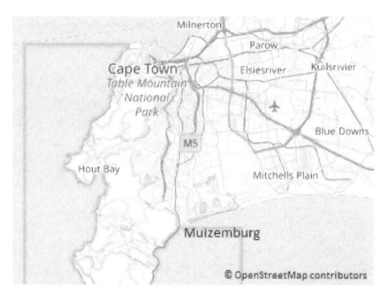

Then Sabrina came by the YMCA to visit me, which I was not expecting, but it was a pleasant surprise. We spent the afternoon together before she left to go back to Port Elizabeth.

Botanist's Tour of Kirstenbosch

On Tuesday the 7th, Julia and Geoff had invited me to a tour the Kirstenbosch National Botanical Gardens situated at the east side of Table Mountain. It had "every" South African plant in it apparently. It was fascinating and made even more so because Geoff was a botanist whose knowledge of the plants greatly added to the tour. I went back to the gardens during my 2017 tour and it was then, during our self-guided tour, that I only fully realised just how much value Geoff's detailed knowledge had added.

I spent a whole day wandering around the gardens with Julia and listening to Geoff. In the evening I went to see the film "Avalanche Express". That was about a CIA agent's plans (Lee Marvin), to use the defection of a Soviet official (Robert Shaw) to kill a Soviet germ-warfare expert on a train. I could guess what was going to happen next long before it did.

7. CAPE TOWN TO WINDHOEK

I want a Mercedes Benz

Unfortunately, the big attraction of Cape Town, Table Mountain, had been covered in cloud since I arrived and still was, so I decided there wasn't much point going up, or waiting a few more days in the hope the weather would clear. I'd continue my travels and hopefully come back for a second try. So, on Wednesday the 8th I set off hitch hiking north from Cape Town up the Western Cape towards South West Africa (that's what the country was called back then, it is called Namibia now).

Why Winhoek? It was an intermediate stop to my true objective, the Skeleton Coast on the edge of the Namib Desert. That was a place that had intrigued me since I had first read about it as a child in my "Look and Learn" children's magazines. . Many ships were wrecked after being pushed there in storms. With no hope of rescue and no access to food and water, all the passengers and crew eventually died and their remains remained there. Hence the name. Their ships lay rotting and rusting like beached whales along the beach. Also the desert had some of the biggest dunes in the world and some of the richest diamond fields ever discovered.

I walked out of the city to get into position on the outskirts. I managed to hitch a lift from Cape Town with Sebastian, who worked in Sales at a top end care dealership in Cape Town. He was probably in his late 20's. He was on his way north to do a round of his rich customers to show off the new Mercedes-Benz E-Class. For me it was a big step up from my £200, 1966, E Reg, beige, but trusty, or should I say rusty, VW Beetle, back in the UK. Well, I like cars, especially top end, well engineered cars, and I remember thinking "what a car". It was so solid and oozed quality. Feeling rather "grand" driving along as a passenger in it, I decided that one day I would have to have a Mercedes too. Took me a while. I eventually had a black one as a company car when I was Head of the Information Systems at an organisation in the mid 1990s. Mind you, in my previous job to that, my company car was a fantastic red BMW 5 Series, so that was close. Superb German engineering! I bought that when I left that firm. The more senior you were the greater the car "reward", "status symbol" and "ego booster" back then before "taxable benefit" eroded the gain.

During the conversation, I told him I was heading up to Windhoek. He looked at me in a very surprised way and said "Really, are you mad?". "Definitely going" I said. He said:-

"There's a bloody war going on up there."

He warned me to be careful I didn't get ambushed. He only went about 40 miles, or so, north to his first appointment, but when we stopped for his turn off, he gave me his business card and said if I returned to Cape Town to give him a call. I could meet up with him and his friends and we'd have a great night out at his favourite night spot, the Pig & Whistle Pub.

The scenery on the way north was spectacular with sea on the left and mountains in the distance on the right. Here's a shot I took

View on the way north from Cape Town

I'm not sure exactly where that view was on the journey up north now.

Damned Clanwilliam

My next lift was with a guy called John who was on his way to north to near the border. He was fascinated by my adventures so far. So, he decided to add to my experiences and took on the role of tour guide when he took a detour to show me the Clanwilliam Dam. He said I should see it as it was impressive. I must confess I was a little perturbed at being driven off the main road by someone I didn't know into an unoccupied area. Thankfully he wasn't a psychopath, just a guy who wanted to proudly show off an impressive feat of engineering. It's on the Olifants River near the town of the same name. The dam provided irrigation water to the downstream Western Cape agricultural region. Here's the photo I took at the time:-

Clanwilliam Dam

After that, plus a "rest stop" in the town of Clanwilliam itself, we set off again driving north up the main highway. As we drove further and further north the country looked increasingly like it had hardly been touched. It was becoming more and more like a beautiful wilderness.

Springbok "Halfway House"

He dropped me off at a hotel close to his destination at a little place called Springbok in the dry Namaqualand area of the Northern Cape province (about 75 miles from the SW African border). I booked into the local hotel and had a pleasant evening playing pool in the bar and drinking beer with some other guys who were also passing through, either travelling north or south. It turned out that Springbok was a popular stop over for travellers between Cape Town and Windhoek. It wasn't quite halfway, but the town and its hotels were among the few places to stop over from then on until Windhoek apparently (he said).

The Rather Scary "Professional Hunter".

On Thursday 9th August after breakfast, I continued on my travels from Springbok and managed to hitchhike all the way to Windhoek, the capital of South West Africa (Namibia), that day via only two lifts:-

Route from Springbok to Windhoek

The first one was with a retired weather-beaten farmer called Bill, who was fascinated by my adventures and plans, and the other was with a tough looking "army type" guy, age about 40 or so, who said he was a "professional hunter". He wasn't a great conversationalist despite my best initial efforts and had a brooding dark and to be frank, rather scary, presence about him. At the time there was a war going on in SW Africa, so I have a suspicion the label he gave himself in conversation of "professional hunter" might have really been a code for "mercenary" or even "regular soldier". The big game areas were inaccessible to tourists due to the war I was told in Windhoek chatting to others later, so his story didn't quite "fit". He had weapons in the car including a pistol in the glove compartment "just in case of hijackings" he said. That was for me to use if needed. He gave it to me after taking the loaded magazine clip out so I could practice with it. He explained that the war was mainly up in the Etosha Pan National Park area north of Windhoek and over the northern border into Angola.

Things really kicked off when Portugal left Angola abruptly, and the country became independent in November 1975. Pro-western UNITA and South African Army forces, with subtle support from the USA he said, were fighting it out with communist MPLA and Cuban troops who were supported by the Soviet Union. It was like a mini extension of the Cold War. Incursion raids and ambushes further south may be possible he added. I was really planning to go north to explore the National Park, but, listening to his strong advice, I decided the risk was rather more than "acceptable". Also, the South African army were road blocking the area, so I probably wouldn't be allowed much further north than Windhoek and anyway, where would I stay? The road was really quiet with hardly any traffic and even fewer signs of human habitation. The semi-arid desert we drove through was beautiful. He was passing Windhoek at about 7pm and said this would be the last place I would be able to get a bed for the night. So, he dropped me off at a hotel on the outskirts of the city on his way through. I was glad that lift was over.

"You can have the caravan out back. It's cheap"

I went into reception at the hotel he had dropped me off at to request a room and they said they were fully booked and there were none. It was on the edge of town, so I had the prospect of walking in the dark into the centre and take my chances there, or trying to hitch a lift. There were other hotels there apparently. However, the receptionist said they had a caravan for hire out the back that was cheap if I wanted to stay there for the night. So, I decide to opt for that rather than risk the walk into town in the dark. With hindsight I think I was probably "being led down the garden path", so to speak. The car park was nowhere near full, the hotel wasn't buzzing like one would be that was full, and the caravan would probably be "off the books". So, the cash I paid up front was probably retained by the receptionist. Should have walked into town. However, you roll the dice and sometimes they don't fall right. More on the consequences of that decision shortly. I dropped my bag off in the caravan which looked old and not particularly clean at all. I found out later it was where "the black servants" slept while "their white bosses" slept in the hotel. Then I left to go to the bar for a drink.

Raffle Tickets for Girls

While I was propping up the hotel bar, I got into conversation with a bloke who introduced himself as Alex. He wouldn't have looked out of place as a cowboy in a western movie. He said he was from Walvis Bay on the Skelton Coast on the other side of the Namib Desert. He told me all about the place and the beautiful desert between Windhoek and there, the diamond mines, shipwrecks on the Skelton Coast, the Germans heritage (it was a German colony until take off them after World War 1 as a spoil of war), diamond mining and the huge sand dunes which were a sight to see. So, I became even more convinced that was my next destination. We had more beers, as he quizzed me about my wanderings to date. Then he said he was heading into town to go to a night club casino in Windhoek on top of Kalahari Sands Hotel and insisted I came along.

He would have already qualified as a "drunk driver" in the UK, but the pair of us piled into his Mercedes, he drove into town along thankfully empty roads, and we went up to the club. He was clearly a "regular" as he was waved straight in and greeted warmly by other guys who were already there. I remember it had a dark "night club" atmosphere inside with dance music playing, not too loud, and a few people were on the dance floor bopping away. The strange thing that gradually hit me was that virtually all the men were white "army types" and the women were virtually all not white, alluringly dressed and quite pretty. Under the apartheid regime and culture of the time that was unusual. It all became clearer when he gave me a book of raffle tickets he's said he had just bought me. He'd already insisted on paying my entrance fee and bought me a beer. So, I thanked him and asked what the raffle tickets were for. He said "for the girls" with a smile. Alex explained that when I "danced" with a girl I paid her in tickets, which they cashed in at the end of the night. That's how they got paid. As I said, he knew loads of guys there. It was clearly a place he was a regular at, so he went off "socialising" and gambling. I stayed propping up the bar pondering my book of tickets and running over the moral question in my head. On the one hand the tickets represented a source of income for the girls. On the other I just didn't want to participate in the "girl activity", as it didn't seem "right" to me – buying a girl's "time".

So, I just propped the bar up and drank beer and continued to take in "the scenery". Eventually Alex joined me at the bar about midnight. He was visibly drunk, and I'd had few too and he was rather perplexed that I handed the unused book of tickets back for him to use next time. The quizzical look on his face clearly indicated a degree of puzzlement about that. I hope I hadn't insulted his generosity, but I probably had. It was time to head back to the hotel. We drove back at high speed and thankfully the road was empty yet again, so Alex didn't crash into anything as we veered onto the wrong side of the road on several occasions. His driving was as drunk as he was. On the way back he said, if I did get to Walvis Bay I was to come and see him (he forgot to give me his address, so that turned out to be rather impossible). He staggered off to his bed and I did the same in the caravan at the rear of the hotel.

Bed Bugs, No Charge

In the morning of the 10th, I woke up to discover I had lots of large red bites on my face (one right smack on the end of my nose), neck, back, hands and arms. They began to itch like hell, and I felt increasingly ill too. I looked like I had bad acne. The climate was hot and dry, so my lips had dried out too. The beer consumption the previous night no doubt helped me sleep through the bed bug attack. After that and hitch hiking just over 1,000 miles in 2 days, I decided I needed a "rest day". After checking out I walked into Windhoek to have a look around. I went to the museum in the Alte Feste (Old Fortress) which was built by Germans when they colonised the country in the 1890's. I went to see the Tintenpalast government building too, and the impressive Christuskirche Lutheran Church, before relaxing, As I sat and watched and listened to the town go by, what was most noticeable was that a lot of the people still spoke German.. Here's some of the photos I took:-

Windhoek museum in the Alte Feste(Old Fortress):
Tintenpalast (Parliament): Christuskirche Lutheran Church

My cracking lips were a worry, so I went into a chemist shop to get something for them and the Pharmacist noticed the lumps and spreading red skin on my face. He was quite concerned about me and asked if it was ok to examine them more closely. I agreed and he confirmed they were bed bug bites which, after I explained where I had been last night, he felt I could only have acquired from that caravan bed. They break through your skin, stick in their proboscis tube and drink your blood apparently. At least I was unaware at the time that I was feeding bed bugs as I'd slept through it thanks to the heavy drinking session. He sold me some pills to take and some cream to put on them that cost me the equivalent of £2.50 [about £13 in 2020]. I booked into a different hotel in the city that night obviously (whose name I failed to note) and, after taking the medication, it made me feel very tired. So, I went to bed early and slept like a log. The itching and sense of feeling ill went within 2 days, but the red lumps stayed for over a week. One of the side effects of the pills was that they continued to make me sleepy, but at least they relieved the itching and swelling.

8. TO THE SKELETON COAST

"The Portuguese"

On the morning of the 11th I hitched from Windhoek heading out north then west across into the Namib Desert towards the Skelton Coast, 220 miles away. There was a route that looked more direct but apparently the one I was on was better made and there was more traffic, as in potential lifts:-

Windhoek to Swakopmund

My first lift took me to the junction to the north of the city where the road split at Okahandja. One road headed north, where my lift, a guy of Portuguese descent, was heading, towards the Etosha National Park and the war, and the other one to the left headed off west through the desert, sign posted for Swakopmund and Walvis Bay. He said he had previously lived in Angola, but had left when Portugal pulled out abruptly and the civil war kicked off. He was meeting some friends in a bar not far from the junction and asked me to join them for a drink, so I did. It was a little bar with two men who he knew sitting on bar stools, plus the barman and us. However, I had a very uneasy feeling about being there. Strange to say, but there was something I felt was instinctively "bad" about them that made me feel very uneasy and increasingly unsafe. I suspect they may have been mercenaries given their "army type" appearance and manner. At that time S Africa and UNITA were employing mercenaries in the bush war apparently. So, I casually said I was just going to the gents which was round the back of the bar next to the rear exit, but instead I continued out the back door and headed quickly back to the road junction. Thankfully, I was relieved to hitch a lift virtually straight away. I had to apologise to the people who picked me up for looking like I hadn't slept in a week and for the multiple bed bug bites all over my face. Unfortunately, they were not going all the way to the coast, but down the road I needed, so I took the lift anyway. About two third of the way to the coast they drove off heading up north in a cloud of dust on a dirt road to their home somewhere out there in the semi-arid desert. It was difficult to imagine how anyone could make a living out there, but perhaps there was a water source they could tap into, or perhaps a mine. So, I found myself standing at that turn off.

Stranded in the Desert

My first thoughts were that I could well be stranded here for some time. We had hardly passed any traffic along the way. I am glad they did drop me off though because it gave me the opportunity to experience the Namib Desert. There was still virtually no traffic at all. Like on the Highveld, on the way to Port Elizabeth, the road was straight. It stretched before me and behind nearly to each horizon. I could see no traffic either way. It was just after mid-day, so, although it was winter, the sun was getting hotter. Fortunately, there was a big square metal road sign on a post about 5 foot off the ground. I can't remember the name of the place they were going to now unfortunately, but the sign was quite useful because, by standing on the east side of it, it provided me with some shade from the sun. I looked around at the sparse desert vegetation and listened to a silence that was total. There was no breeze, no bird song, no animal noises, just utter silence. That was another marvellous experience.

Mad Dogs and Englishmen

I'm not sure how long after being dropped off it was, but it felt like hours later when I eventually heard the low rumble of an engine noise far off in the distance and the glint of a windscreen coming gradually towards me. I had started to wonder if I was going to have to stay there into the night. I thought "I had better get this lift, or I'm in big trouble". The car came along, I stuck my thumb out, smiled and it stopped. The driver leaned over and rolled the passenger window down. He said, "Where are you heading", in a German sounding English accent. So, I said "to the coast", so he said, "jump in". Turned out he was a Swiss national called Hans working in country, although on what and where he never said. I suspect, that being Swiss, he was in the diamond industry which was big on the coast. When I got in and he drove off he sang a line jokingly to me, from a song by Noel Coward:

"Mad dogs and Englishmen go out in the midday sun" .

By that, he meant "what was I doing standing out in the middle of the desert in the midday sun? Was I nuts?" It was a dangerous thing to do he said, because if I got sunstroke, there was no chance of getting medical help in time. It was not so bad though, because the road sign had given me shade. Plus, it was winter, so although it was hot by UK standards, it was nowhere near as hot as it would have been in the summer. At least that's what I told myself anyway.

9. SPRECHEN SIE DEUTSCH?

Swakopmund Strand

Anyway, he arrived late in afternoon at Swakopmund and dropped me off at a "nice hotel" called The Strand Hotel built on a spit of land that jutted out into the sea:-

The Strand Hotel, Swakopmund

I accepted his recommendation and booked in for two nights. It was very nice. The town of Swakopmund had been built by Germany when South West Africa was a German colony [called Südwestafrika] in 1884. It remained German until it was successfully invaded by a combined British and South African army in 1915. It was officially ceded under the Treaty of Versailles in 1919 after the end of World War 1 to be run under a League of Nations Mandate by the Union of South Africa [until it became independent in 1990]. Many people were still descendants of the original settlers and German was spoken quite commonly by African and white people. The architecture was very much Germanic in style too. It looked like a normal pretty seaside town between the sea and the edge of the desert.

"This is my daughter Dominique"

In the evening I went into the hotel bar for a drink. I was propping the bar up by myself chatting to the SW African barman, who eloquently spoke both English and German, about the Skeleton Coast, shipwrecks, and the diamond mining operations. It was there that a middle-aged man, called John, opened a conversation with me when he came to the bar to buy drinks for his group. He said he was British too and had spotted my accent. So, he started chatting and asked me what I was doing. So, I said, "hitch hiking around Southern Africa" and, on request, started to give him a quick summary of where I had been so far. I must have stimulated his curiosity because part way through my oration he interjected and insisted I joined his group for dinner. It was a bit daunting, but I accepted.

That was the thing about hitch hiking. Many of the people who gave me a lift wanted to buy me a meal, or a drink, or both, with no hidden agenda. It restores your faith in human nature. I guess they saw "cash strapped student" and I also think many probably wished they could have done, or do, something similar. A frequent typical comment was

> *"God man, you've seen more of the country than I have, and I have lived here all my life".*

John had also overheard some of my conversation with one of the barman as he waited his turn to be served. So, he whispered to me as we wandered from the bar to the restaurant area that it was better if I did not ask questions or talk about diamond mining, because I might attract the attention of the local police. They were always on the lookout for potential diamond smugglers and associated types, and they didn't mess about, so I really didn't want to get into a tangle with them.

Anyway, he guided me over to his table and sat me in the only free chair between him and his daughter, Dominique. He introduced me to the others, his wife and his daughter's friend and her boyfriend, who were all keen to know about me and my adventures. So, I reeled off where I'd been etc. Later, I learnt that my host was the managing director of a British subsidiary supplying the mining industry. His daughter Dominique was blond and, well, yes, very beautiful and attractive, aged about 20, or so. She worked for a small airline, which a little internet searching while writing this suggests it might have been Namib Air. We got on well. At the end of a lovely meal the bill arrived, and I tried to pay my share and John would have none of it. He insisted on picking up everything. I thanked him greatly. After they were all going back to John's house and insisted I should come along too. The house was located along the seafront. It was German in style and very large and beautiful. After a drink in the living room John and his wife bade their good nights to go to bed, but said to us to stay if we liked. Dominique, her friend, and boyfriend were keen to continue the night and carry-on drinking and chatting. There was even a discussion about going out again to a local bar that would still be open. I was tired though, so had to say a fond goodnight to Dominique and her friends and left to walk back along the deserted sea front to the hotel and some much needed sleep. The bed bug bites and pills were still affecting me, and I wasn't feeling great. I suspected that the medication was making me drowsy too, ably assisted by the beer and wine. With hindsight I should have stayed on as requested, but there's no going back now.

The Incredible Dunes!!

On the 12th I'd actually slept like a log overnight and didn't wake up until very late the next morning. As I said, it would have been the pills mixed with much alcohol, I guess. I was way too late for breakfast, but I didn't feel overly keen on eating anyway. I spent the rest of the day exploring the area by foot. Swakopmund was sandwiched between the Namib Desert and the sea. Spurred on by my conversations with Alex in Windhoek, I had a walk about in the German style town itself, then set off south walking along the sea front next to the highway towards Walvis Bay. When I had virtually lost sight of the town itself the rocky outcrops gave way to a sandy beach that looked like it stretched for miles. The desert sand dunes were right next to the road. I just could not resist heading at right angles from the sea, across the highway, and straight into the Namib Desert. Here's a photo I took:-

Namib Desert

It's been slightly scratched with the passage of time, so the marks you can see are "added features". The amazing thing about the sand dunes was their sheer size. Some were enormous with maybe 100+ foot tall ridges and formed a barrier that I had to breach if I was to explore the vast Namib Desert beyond them. The dunes ran parallel to the coast in rows like waves coming towards a beach. So, to make progress I had little choice but to climb the dunes. When I reach the crest of the first dune, I could see more rows stretching back about a couple of miles back and then beyond them there appeared to be sparse desert as far as I could see to the horizon. The dunes reminded me of those in the film, Lawrence of Arabia. They were quite a sight. Once on a dune's crest I could walk north along it for a while basically heading back in the rough direction of town, then skid down the other side into the trough and then on up and down other dunes and so on. It was harder than I expected because every time you climbed a step up, you slipped back half a step, so it was quite difficult to get to the crests, but it was very easy, and fun, to leap down the other side.

Eventually the dunes ended, and flatter desert began. I crossed a dirt track that ran parallel to the dunes, it looked like a north-south back road between Walvis Bay and Swakopmund, and then as I walked further into the desert, it felt increasingly like I could be the first human to walk there for some time, if ever. I could see no signs of prior human activity at all anywhere. It's not very often you get the chance to be somewhere like that. Special.

A Desert Rose

One of the most amazing things that I found on my little adventure that day were little Desert Roses. That's not the name of a plant. It's a stone formation formed from rock crystals that often looks like a rose. Some were about the size of a clenched fist. I brought one of the better ones back to remind me of that special time wandering in the wilderness. Here's a photo of it next to a 2020 UK 5p coin for perspective: -

Desert Rose

I had not heard about the roses beforehand and had no idea at the time how they were formed, but they were beautiful to see. However, the friendly bar man filled me in on the details and solved the mystery later that evening. Jenny and David did too on my arrival back in Jo'burg,

"Desert roses are a crystal formation made from evaporates formed in wet sand by an inflow of water containing dissolved minerals which evaporation leaving crystals behind".

So, I guess that they are probably formed as a consequence of the dense fog that rolled into the desert from the Atlantic Ocean virtually every day before the sun burnt it off. Eventually, being aware of the impending darkness as the sun dipped closer to the horizon to the west ,I headed NW and eventually intersected that dirt track and headed north towards Swakopmund. That night I went to bed early, which was unusual for me. I was very tired. That was still probably due a possible infection from the bed bug bites and the drugs the chemist had given me for them to alleviate the itching.

Walvis Bay In and Out

On Monday the 13th of August it was time to check out of the hotel and leave Swakopmund. So, after breakfast, which I managed to get to in time, unlike the previous day, I hitched a lift down south to Walvis Bay. Unlike the picturesque Swakopmund it was closer to a functional industrial and working "fishing port" type place set out in grid pattern, like Swakopmund, so not with as much architectural "tourist appeal":-

Walvis Bay

In those days the port was officially part of South Africa, but there was no border evident as such between there and Swakopmund. Not a surprise really, given that both countries were run by South Africa.

After a short sightseeing wander around I decided not to stop any longer and to hitch all the way back to Windhoek that day 245 miles away. I'd been warned previously it would be prudent not to venture down the Skelton Coast past Walvis Bay into the main diamond mining area. I might be mistaken for a potential diamond thief and get arrested. Sounded like that might be true, so my rational self-won the internal battle, and I took on board the advice. It's a shame really because I was looking forward to seeing that area. So, getting back to Windhoek involved retracing my previous journey.

I'm not sure where I took this picture, but given its sequence on the film it is likely to be the Walvis Bay Lagoon given the flamingos in the water:-
e

Walvis Bay Lagoon

Stranded by Uranium Mine

I had my first lift out of Walvis Bay on a worker's bus that drove back through Swakopmund and east back the way I came towards Windhoek. The driver dropped me off at the Arandis crossroads where he was turning off for the Rossing Uranium Mine to the south. That put me well into the Namib Desert. The other problem was that by then time was getting on. It was about 4:30pm and there was about 2 hours of day light left. Arandis, at 2 miles away to the north, was in the wrong direction for Windhoek.

In the days before the internet, I had no access to any information on how big Arandis was. So, I didn't know if there was a guest house, or hotel, there. There were no mobile phones either, so that was out too. Rather than risk it, I decided to continue hitching from where I was. I stood there for ages, and it soon became clear that I was in for a long wait. Hardly any vehicles used the road, so I decided my only chance was to start walking east further into the desert along the road towards Windhoek.

I hoped would get there before it got too cold. It gets cold in the desert at night. I wrote in my diary that I thought it was 20 miles away but what I did not comprehend was that was really 200 miles away:-

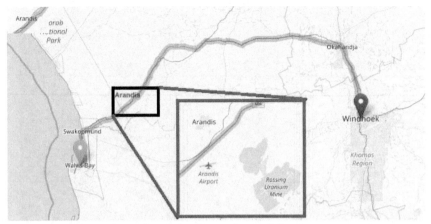

Source: OpenStreetMap

"Give me my Coke back!"

After about one hour of walking, I heard the noise of a vehicle engine increasing in volume from behind me. There's hardly any noise in the desert so noise travels. I waited, hoping it would stop. Thumb out, smile on. Turns out it was an open backed run down and battered van. It stopped. He was going to Windhoek too, so I was lucky. Very lucky. I was about to open the passenger door to climb in when the driver indicated with his thumb and a few unintelligible words, probably in German, to jump into the back of the van.

There were already 3 guys (perhaps also hitchhikers) on the back, two were black and one white. The wind was blowing round us badly as we sped along. Before the sun set it was quite warm but, as soon it went down, it quickly became very cold and felt even colder due to the wind chill effect. I arrived in Windhoek 2 hours after sunset at about 8.30pm. By then I was literally shaking with the cold. Still, that's better than getting stuck in the desert.

I remember something quite fascinating about that drive. I offered the two black guys my can of Coke for a drink, thinking it was a "take a swig, pass it round". They took it, but didn't pass it round, or give it to the other white guy, who I assumed would then take a drink and pass it back to me to finish what was left over. I had only had a couple of swigs from it. The other white guy offered them a smoke and they took a cigarette each, but they smoked one together and kept the other one for later. Eventually I told the black guys in English supplemented by "sign language", as I didn't speak German, to "give me my Coke back please", which they did. The other white guy then told me that if you offer one the members of their tribe anything they keep it and don't give it back. It is their custom. You have given it to them as a gift to keep. I suppose they thought I was being very bad mannered when I asked for it back.

When I arrived back in Windhoek, I booked myself into the same hotel as before in the centre, had a couple of strong drinks in the bar to get my system working again, had a bath and then I gladly dropped into bed.

10. SURREAL DASH TO CAPE TOWN

Armed Protector

On the 14th August I was up and in the hotel restaurant the moment it opened at 7am for breakfast. I'd decided to head back to Cape Town, some 920 miles away: -

Windhoek to Cape Town

I really hoped to get up Table Mountain, minus clouds. By 8am I was in place on the edge of Windhoek hitchhiking where I was joined by a white South Africa soldier called Francois. He was going on leave and hitchhiking home to his parents' farm near Kimberley from the war zone up north. Half his route coincided with mine, so we decided to hitch together. I was quite happy about that because Francois was wearing his army kit and carrying his rifle, so he effectively provided me with armed protection. Whilst the war up north was largely just happening "up there", that wasn't to say incursions weren't a possibility. He clearly thought so. We kept hitching throughout the day. At one point we managed to get a lift offer with some locals who wanted paying before they would let us in their car. Francois told me he had said, "Thanks, but no thanks", in Afrikaans and just walked off. I took his lead and followed. Some words were shouted as us as they sped off in a language I couldn't understand, and given the associated hand gestures I probably couldn't record here anyway. Other (free) lifts followed and by about 5.30pm we had hitch hiked over 300 miles south to the B1-B4 junction. We had to get out of our lift there because they were carrying on west along the B1 and we were both heading south. That junction was just after a little town called Keetmanshoop:-

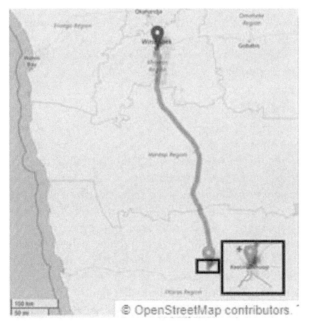

© OpenStreetMap contributors.

Windhoek to Keetmanshoop

We waited and waited for a vehicle to pass. The only place in the UK that I have been to that reminded me a little of there was the north west coast of Scotland at Cape Wrath, which is very sparsely populated. We were still standing there at the junction trying to get a lift at well after the sun had set. We were on a slight rise so you could see a few twinkling lights in Keetmanshoop 3 miles or so away back up the road we had just travelled down and that was it. Now the sensible thing to do would have been to walk back to the town and look for some accommodation for the night, but Francois was keen to get home on leave as quickly as he could, so we decided to continue hitching. The night was cold, and the sky was completely clear because of the absence of any humidity in the desert air and the lack of light from human habitation.

The Amazing Milky Way

Looking up I could see the most amazing array of stars. There really is a "milky way" spanning the sky in a band corresponding to the spiral galaxy we are a minute grain of sand within. There were literally millions of stars visible in the sky packed so closely together that they gave the appearance of a milky band right over the top of you from horizon to horizon. Many times more stars than I had ever seen before, or since. It was a spectacular sight and one I will never forget.

There literally were no vehicles heading in any direction. You could see for miles as the road was, as I said, on a bit of a rise, so it was clear there were no head lights heading our way any time soon. Time dragged on and on until about midnight.

"Halt, or I WILL Shoot"

It was just after that that I had, what felt at the time, like a real brush with genuine danger. We could see two vehicles in convoy coming towards us down the road from the north with lights on full beam. When they were about 50 yards away, they stopped side by side across the road facing us leaving their lights on full beam. That pretty much blinded us. All we could see through the glare were the silhouettes of about 10 men pile out of the front and back of the vehicles and start walking in a line down the road towards us. Francois, the soldier I was hitching with, whispered to me that they were black Africans. He could tell that from the language and accent they were talking in, which we could hear as they came on towards us. Some of them were holding bottles in their hands and by their silhouettes, swagger, and demeanour it was clear they were in uniform, had been drinking and several were drunk. It brought an image into my head of the many westerns I had watched as a child. Outlaws lined up walking towards their inevitable gun fight. Francois was clearly in fear for our safety given his heightened sense of alertness and immediate reaction. He readied his rifle and asked me if I had a weapon. I said I had a knife (it was only a pen knife so I'm not sure what good that would have done). He told me to quickly open it and I tucked it down my trouser belt behind me. Just in case. When they were about 20 yards off Francois cocked his rifle. It made quite a distinctive click clack click sound in the still night. He brought it up so it was pointing towards them and said in Afrikaans "Stop, of ek skietin" [which he said afterwards meant "Halt, or I will shoot"] That made them stop dead in their tracks. We were lit up by the vehicle lights and partially blinded by them too. After a couple of seconds, one of them took a step forward very slowly holding both hands up, so we could see them, shouting ""Nee skiet, my soldaat" in Afrikaans ["No shoot, me soldier"].. There was an exchange between Francois and the group as he conversed to them a firm "no messing" tone Afrikaans voice. Then, when he had heard enough and he was happy with the replies, he nodded and turned to me. He said they were African soldiers in the South West African Army and so were on "our side", but he added quietly, that he didn't entirely trust them, so we were going to stay calm, friendly, but to be very wary. The soldier who had spoken first edged forward and, bowing a little, shook hands with Francois and then me, smiling broadly. Then the rest all came forward slowly and shook hands. I tell you, it seemed like a close thing at the time. We both thought we were in for trouble. I couldn't understand any of the Afrikaans conversations that took place, but from the tone it seemed amicable enough. So, I just held back on the side making sure none of them were behind me, looked like I "understood" and waited.

They had all drunk from bottles of something alcoholic, so they were quite merry. They offered us drinks, but Francois said "nee danki" ("no thanks") and whispered to me to say the same, which I did. He said he had told them we were looking for a lift south. There was more conversation until, after what felt like ages, but it was probably only a few minutes, Francois indicated for me to follow him as we walked back up the road following the group back to their vehicles. They turned out to be army Land Rovers. Francois and I got into the first one with some of the black soldiers and the rest piled into the other one. They headed south in the direction we wanted to go. They'd agreed to give us a lift to the next "town" apparently, which was great.

It didn't take us more than 200 yards to realise our driver was clearly drunk, or a bad driver, or both. The Land Rover gradually veered to and fro onto the wrong side of the road and back and occasionally onto the verge edge kicking up dust . Thankfully there was virtually no traffic on the road south at that time in the early hours of the morning. The "fun" wasn't over though. In the distance we would see a massive American style "road train" truck, fully lit up, coming towards us. Our driver was thankfully concentrating hard trying to focus on keeping the Land Rover on the right side of the road and thank God, he managed it, although it was a bit too close for comfort.

After about 100 miles and 2 hours later in the early hours we arrived at the next little settlement of Grunow.

Grunow

Francois could have continued with them as they were going in his direction for another 60 miles or so, but he had had enough "fun" for one night he said, so decide to quit while he was ahead ….. and alive. It was there that Francois and I parted company. He was going east along the road to his parent's farm near Kimberley [still over 400 miles away to the east]. So, he wished me luck, shook hands, and walked off in that direction to get into position to hitch his next lift. I started to walk south west along the road to keep warm. It ran along the edge of Grunow. It was freezing that night in the desert, so walking helped me to maintain some heat.

Sheep Truck to Cape Town

It was something like 2am by then on the 15th August. An enormous lorry, at least twice the ;emght of anything you would see in the UK at that time, had stopped by the side of the road. Judging by the smell and animal noises coming from the trailers they were transporting live sheep. A dim light was on inside the cab, and I could just about see the occupants. So, I thought, no point bleating about it, might as well try for a lift. So I sheepishly tapped on the driver's side door, the window wound down, a head popped out and he was clearly more than a bit shocked and surprised to see anyone that time of night in the middle of nowhere, let alone a hitch hiker from the UK. Smile…. thumb up…. politely ask him if there was any chance of a lift, as I was heading to Cape Town. He said he was going there too, so climb in. I couldn't believe my luck. The driver, Pieter, was white, probably Afrikaner judging from the accent and name, or maybe of German descent, and his co-driver was black. Pieter didn't introduce me to his black colleague, so I did that myself, and he nodded and smiled back. That was probably an indication of "normal" racial relations where blacks were treated by some as "there, but not there" in the way I imagine a

Victorian might interact a house servant. Pieter called and referred to the black guy as "Boy" even though he was probably in his 30's at a guess, and he in turn always replied, "Ja Boss". I'm not sure he understood English that well. Anyway, they prepared to re-start the journey, fired up the massive engine and we rolled out south leaving Grunow behind. They took turns driving through the night as they continued their journey to deliver a cargo of live sheep to market in Cape Town the following day.

There was a narrow 2 foot "bed" to the rear of the cab behind the seats that spanned the full width of the cabin. So, Pieter said I should catch a little sleep back there between his turn driving. The other shocking thing was that when I woke up Pieter was driving, so I indicated to the black guy if he wanted to use the bed, but Pieter said "no" firmly to me and didn't translate what he said to our black companion but judging by the tone it was a negative to sleeping on the bed. Pieter said to me that he had to make do with sleeping on the passenger seat. That was apartheid in microcosm. They drove all through the night until 7am when the engine started to misfire and so we had to stop. Pieter found that the fuel line had started to leak. I could tell from the colourful language that this was clearly serious. He said he had no idea how long it would take to fix and, after a pause and a head scratch, suggested it would be better if I tried to press on and if he caught up with me later, he would pick me up again. So, I said my thanks to both and continued to walk along the road to find a suitable place to hitch another lift.

Donkey Collision, Smashed Head

Only a short while later and a few hundred yards down the road, a car pulled up with two white guys in it and the driver's front side and bonnet was badly crumpled and had clearly impacted something at speed. The window wound down and the driver said:-

"Hey, can you drive man, I've crashed and
smashed my head?"

By the look of it, the damage to his forehead should have put him out cold. His passenger wasn't any better. Not a little taken aback I asked where they were heading, and they said they were going all the way to a little place not far from Cape Town. They explained that they had hit and killed a donkey during the night at about 75mph. The cracks in the wind screen were where the driver's head had contacted the glass. So much for wearing a seat belt. Do I need to say the donkey was sent flying and very dead through the air? It turned out they were a couple of tough fishermen who had just made R10,000 during 3 months on a fishing boat out of Walvis Bay they said. In 1979, at R1.85 to £1, that was the equivalent of about £5,000-6,000, (or about £25,000 in 2020). So, the driver stumbled out and fell into the back and I took the driver's seat and off I drove.

Anyway, that went off without a hitch so to speak, even though I was tired myself and I was expecting the engine to start making funny noises or the steering to fail at any point. I could still see through the cracked windscreen and there was nothing else on the road. I tried to persuade them to get medical attention, but they weren't bothered and clearly, they felt they were far too tough for such niceties. I pulled up at their turnoff just after dawn. I didn't catch their names and there wasn't much conversation. They thanked me for taking the strain for a while and drove off, heading left to their destination which wasn't that much further apparently.

As I stood there watching their car disappear into the distance it felt like I'd been in a crazy movie, first the milky way, then the incident with the soldiers and that scary encounter, the sheep truck saga with John and his co-driver, topped off nicely by those two injured souls and the dead donkey.

As the dawn progressed into morning, traffic picked up slightly and it wasn't long at all before my next lift stopped and kindly took me a little closer to Cape Town. I could see Table Mountain looming larger on the horizon in the left photo below. The second lift took me even closer before they dropped me off at their turn off, so I could see both Table Mountain and Cape Town across the bay and to my delight there was still no cloud covering the top: -

Approach to Cape Town from the north

After a thankfully totally uneventful lift, I eventually arrived back in Cape Town at 2.30pm. I had covered 920 miles in about just over 30 hours without a break and only fitful sleep for a short while in the back of the sheep truck. Quite a ride, was it not?

Table Mountain. I didn't want to come down.

I decided to go straight up Table Mountain that afternoon by cable car without delay because, if you recall, the first time I was there it was covered in cloud. That day the weather was perfect. But I didn't want to tempt fate. So, I made my way to the cable car station, paid the fare, and rode up to the top. It was so clear; I had some beautiful views from up there: -

I didn't want to come down really, but I had check into the YMCA again. Obviously, I had hitched a hell of a long way over the last two days (just over 1,600 miles), so I was tired by then. It's no surprise then that I noted in my diary that I should have had an early night to catch up on some sleep. But I didn't.

Pig & Whistle... Again

If you recall, one of the lifts I had had when I was leaving Cape Town to go to Windhoek, was with a up market car salesman called Sebastian who gave me his card. He said to call him if I came back, so I did. He said he was going out that evening with a bunch of friends, so I arranged to meet at the Pig and Whistle pub at 7pm. I had a great time. There was a nice blonde girl Sebastian had brought along called Suzie and he introduced us. I got on well with her, but after a few beers I uncharacteristically had to call it a night just after 10pm. I was having difficulty staying awake. So, I made my excuses to Suzie, Sebastian, and his other friends, with regret, and left to get some much-needed sleep.

11. MARATHON HITCH HIKE TO JO'BURG

Up and Away at the Crack of Dawn

On Thursday the 16th August I rose early, checked out of the YMCA, and had started to hitch by 7am. I got my first lift from a guy called Dave for 75 miles to his hometown of Worcester. That's on the other side of the mountains north-east of Cape Town on the N1 highway north to Johannesburg in the wine region. Dave had told me all about the superb wines they made there and how beautiful the place was. I should have stopped longer, booked into a hotel, sample much local produce and explored the region some more, but I didn't. Why? No idea now. I did manage to come back to the wine region during my 2017 tour though and more than filled that gap.

I must go to bed. You can join me if you want?

My second lift was on a lorry driven by Ben, who was heading to Jo'burg. He drove all though the day until nearly midnight until we reached Britstown in the Karoo. He said he was going to have to go to bed in the 2-foot-wide bed that spanned the width of the cab behind the seats and added that I was very welcome to join him if I felt like it. That came as a bit of a "surprise", so I politely declined, mumbled something about needing to get on, but thanked him anyway, as I simultaneously opened the door, and jumped out. Everywhere in Britstown was closed, including any potential overnight accommodation and nobody was about. So, I walked to the east edge of town, and I started hitching again... just after midnight!

Cape Town to Britstown

That's the route so far. I had an expectation that I was going to be stranded by the roadside all through the cold night waiting for a lift. I was lucky again with the hitch hiking though, because, within minutes, a lone car appeared driving my way and the driver, called Simon, stopped.

Breakdown at Potchefstroom

He was going all the way to Jo'burg. He drove through that night, and I managed to sleep a little in the car, but it was not easy to sleep on a bumpy road.

Britstown to Potchefstroom

I "missed" Kimberley completely when we drove through while it was dark. I must have nodded off. Kimberley was on my "must see" list as I had read about its diamond mining history. Cecil Rhodes made his fortune there too and I was aware of the long siege of British forces during the Second Anglo-Boer war (1899-1900). However, Simon's luck ran out mid-day on Friday, 17th August, when something went wrong with his engine at Potchefstroom. By then I'd covered some 800 miles since leaving Cape Town the previous morning.

He went into town to see if he could find a mechanic, so I said my thanks, wished him luck and went to hitch another lift. Literally, within 2 seconds, as I stuck my thumb out, a car pulled up. He was going to Jo'burg too, about another 75 miles further on, so I jumped in. He kindly dropped me off right at my destination at the university at about 3pm. I went to see if David was around, who, by pure luck, happened to be in his office. Remember those were the days before everyone had a mobile phone. I didn't want to disrupt his work as he was clearly busy, so I left and walked round to Julia's apartment in the inner city affluent residential area of Hillbrow and she was in.

"Unknown guy in bath at girlfriend's apartment "

Looking back with hindsight, that visit to Julia's was a surreal experience. When I arrived, Julia asked me if I would like a bath. I can't figure out why I didn't think that was unusual, but at the time, I thought "oh, I've just travelled back from Cape Town without a break, so perhaps I'm a bit sweaty?". Anyway …. I thanked her and went into the bathroom, stripped off and jumped into the bath. I was soaking in the water when I heard the doorbell. Julia "whispered" anxiously to tell me her boyfriend had arrived. He clearly wasn't expected. There was a bit of a "discussion" in the living room while I dried myself off and dressed. When I came out there was a bit of an atmosphere. It wasn't the same guy I had met in Cape Town. I found out later it was her "Jo'burg boyfriend", John. I think I was a little naïve then. But I didn't say anything about Cape Town. Julia clearly had a complicated love life. Also "unknown guy in bath at girlfriend's apartment" wasn't a "good look" was it?

Anyway, I didn't stay very long after John arrived and made my rapid excuses and set off on the way back to The Little House in Bez Valley. There were some welcome letters from home waiting for me. Then I went back to the "PiG" for a few drinks and then out for a Chinese with Jenny and David later that evening. That meal only cost me the equivalent of 65p in 1979 money = £3.35 in 2020 - fantastic value.

4,685 Miles So far

At that point I had covered about 4,685 miles rambling around southern Africa, so on Saturday the 18th August I decided to spend the day relaxing, reading, sunbathing, writing some letters, updating Jenny and David on my travels, and generally doing nothing much.

12. JO'BURG TO VICTORIA FALLS

The Smoke That Thunders

Having read stories of Dr Livingstone's adventures when I was a boy I hankered after seeing the great Victoria Falls. I'd learnt that the local Klolo-Lozi tribe called the falls "Mosi-oa-Tunya", which translates as "the smoke that thunders". That's a pretty accurate description of the sight that awaited me. On Sunday the 19th August, I played squash with David (much better this time), then everyone came to The Little House for a Braii at tea time.

One of the guys from the PiG was there called Giles, the one I asked about Julia. He was from Zimbabwe-Rhodesia himself and doing a post grad at the university We chatted about the place, how to get to the Falls and so on. Then, to my surprise, he said he was, in fact, heading up that way first thing tomorrow morning, Monday the 20th, to Musina on the Zimbabwe-Rhodesian border and would I like a lift? An opportunity too good to pass by. So, I said "yes" immediately. He was doing some research up there apparently along the Zambezi River. That flows along the border between Zimbabwe-Rhodesia and South Africa, or should I say the border is demarcated by the river and his base, Musina, was located near the confluence of the Limpopo and Sand Rivers.

So, the next day, Giles rolled up at The Little House in his car at 7am and off we went. After a clear uneventful drive, we arrived at Musina around 2.30pm. Giles took me on a drive to see the Limpopo River. I was expecting a "River Nile" like experience, but it was as dry as a bone. It was the dry season: We walked out into the middle of the river bed which, as I said, was the border between South Africa and Zimbabwe-Rhodesia. It would have been quite easy to cross if we had wanted to, although probably rather risky given that a Bush War was underway on the Zimbabwe-Rhodesian side.

Here's Giles and I standing in the middle of the Limpopo River:-

Myself (left) and Giles

The dry bed of the Limpopo.

After that little trip, Giles said he was going to the stables for a bit of horse riding through the bush and would I like to join him. So, I said "great, yes". Off we went for a couple of hours until the sun set into the Bush. Good fun, but I'd never ridden a horse before for that length of time, so my bum was a bit sore the following day. The nearest I'd come to horse riding was on the little ponies at the seaside at 6d for a saunter round the ring. The horse probably decided he wasn't going to tolerate a complete amateur, so he dragged me between two thorn bushes and left me with scratches down my sides . You should have heard my language just after that. It's a good job the horse didn't understand English. African thorn bushes are much more lethal than their UK cousins. After that little incident I made sure he went exactly where I wanted him to.

After we arrived back at the stables the sun was setting, and Giles took a shot of me:-

Horse riding by the border

Kicked out of Zimbabwe-Rhodesia

Musina is only a short distance from the border and the nearest Zimbabwe-Rhodesian town of Beitbridge, so Giles and another friend of his decided to pop over there for supper and took me along. We arrived at the South African Customs, and they let us through with no bother, but the Zimbabwe-Rhodesian Immigration Officer wouldn't let me in. He said I had no proof that I had a return ticket to Britain. He even made me a "Prohibited Person" which is usually only allotted to terrorists, criminals and such like, Giles said. Not many people can claim to have had one of those. I proudly kept that "Notice of Prohibited Person" form they gave me as a souvenir: -

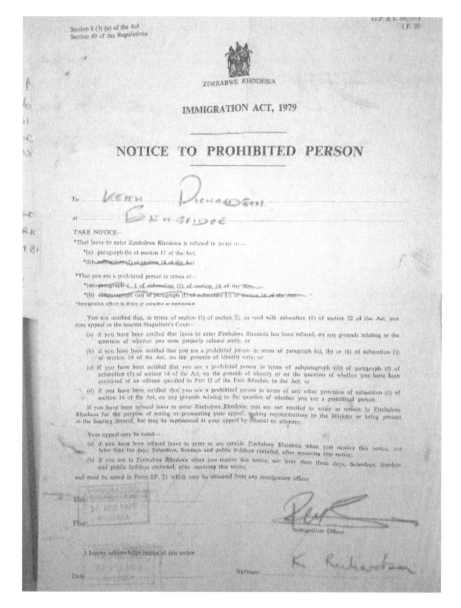

So instead, we all did a U turn back to the South African side and went to Giles' friends' place for a meal.

"Papers please"

Having talked about the problem with Giles and his friend, it was decided that the best way to get round the Prohibited Person Order was to get proof of my return flight to the UK. But how to do that without me going all the way back to Jo'burg, or asking the airline to post something to Giles in a couple of days or so? There was a travel agent in Musina, so we decided the best option was to go to them in the morning and see if there was a way they could help.

So as soon as they were open on the 21st, I went there and they couldn't do enough for me, they were so helpful. They contacted South African Airways who confirmed my ticket details, and the agent was then able to give me an official looking document to prove I had a return ticket to fly back to the UK and when that was. That meant I was able to use that to gain entry to Zimbabwe-Rhodesia.

The agent also said,

"You do realise that there is a Bush War going on over the border, don't you?"

He strongly advised me to fly to Victoria Falls and avoid the road between there and Bulawayo as vehicles were being ambushed and people killed. He explained that he happened to have a package holiday available, including flights from Bulawayo to Victoria Falls return and 2 nights' accommodation at the famous Victoria Falls Hotel for R150, the equivalent of about £80 back then or £430 in 2021. An absolute bargain, he said. So, I bought it.

Having sorted that out, I met up with Giles and he drove me up to the border, aiming for 11am. We had some spare time, so before we crossed, we went to have a look further up the Limpopo at a large rock pool that was full of water:-

Limpopo

We were hoping to see some crocodiles and hippos, Giles said, but we were out of luck. They must have been hiding. Then we drove over the border crossing to Beitbridge. Obviously, it was moment of tension as the Immigration Officer looked at me in that penetrating way he had obviously honed from years of practice, probably thinking "Oh, it's you again is it!". My luck was in, because instead of telling me to turn around and walk back to South Africa, as I was a "Prohibited Person", he just said, "Papers please". I handed my passport over, plus the proof of my UK flight ticket and Victoria Falls holiday package papers. After examining them a little too carefully, for what seemed at the time, like ages, but probably only a few seconds, the Officer granted me access and brought the required stamp crashing down onto my passport with a thump. After that Giles took me to a local hotel known as "Peter's Motel", for lunch. The owner was a friend of his. I had fillet steak, which was very nice.

"Talking Shit"

Over lunch Giles told me an interesting, as well as funny, story. He said the Africans round there gave all the whites individual nicknames. Well, there was a policeman in Musina who was always pulling the locals in and asking them questions. The name they'd given him when translated into English was "Talking Shit", because every time they answer one of his questions he replied, "You're talking shit, man". So, they called him that. Giles said his African name was the word for "Beard"…because he had a beard.

Creative Currency Conversion

Giles also explained that transferring currency out of Zimbabwe-Rhodesia was very difficult. He had money in a bank there in Beitbridge. So, we had already worked out how much I was likely to spend in Zimbabwe-Rhodesia and I had paid him the equivalent of that in Rands on the South African side of the border. He withdrew the cash from his bank in Beitbridge in Zimbabwe-Rhodesia currency and gave that to me.

"Can you shoot?"

Now in those days, as I said, there was a "Bush War" going on in Zimbabwe-Rhodesia between the white led government and various supporters and black terrorists of ZANU and ZAPO, as we called them then, or freedom fighters, depending on your perspective. It didn't end until December 1979, so I had arrived just before the end of it. Ambushes between urban areas were a continual threat during the war. So, the Zimbabwe-Rhodesians had an armed convoy system in operation where all traffic was queued up at the Beitbridge border, then escorted by the army in very heavily armed armoured vehicles. The guy who gave me a lift to Bulawayo called them "Gun Ships", but I think with further research they were also called "Crocodiles" given the similarity of their shape to that reptile. It was a longer distance photo that I took, but here's a "Gun Ship" waiting at the front of the convoy.

Convoy Gun Ship

They were specially designed vehicles higher above the ground than usual and shaped so that if a mine went off under the wheels the explosive force should be mainly deflected and reduce the impact and injuries to the occupants

In my case, I needed to get a lift in the only armed convoy leaving at 1pm for Bulawayo so I could link up with my package holiday flight in Bulawayo the following day. After thanking Giles and his friend for an excellent lunch I started walking along the long line of cars waiting to set off in the convoy.

One thing that instantly struck me was that it felt like I was walking along a 1960s car rally. Rhodesia's 300,000, or thereabouts, white inhabitants had made a Unilateral Declaration of Independence (UDI) way back in 1964 to avoid British imposed independence and the black majority rule that would have resulted (black population circa 6 million). Since then, sanctions had been deployed internationally against them that hindered the import of many things, including cars. So, it appeared to me that many vehicles from the 1960s were kept going long after they might have been scrapped elsewhere. The climate also helped keep rust away too of course. As a quick aside the Prime Minister of Rhodesia since 1964 was Ian Smith. His mother, Agnes Hodgson, was born in Cumberland not far from where I grew up. He was an RAF fighter pilot officer during World War 2 too.

Here's a photo I took standing next to my lift just before we set off on the 210 mile journey to Bulawayo:-

Waiting for the convoy to set off

I talked to the soldiers standing at the rear of the armed convoy by their "Gun Ship" to find out whether I could jump in with them, hoping for a 'yes'. They said the best thing to do was to just walk along past each of the 50 or so vehicles in turn wiggling my hitch-hiking thumb to indicate I was looking for a lift and someone was bound to oblige. So, I did that, but I wasn't having much luck with most occupants avoiding my "look", or shaking their heads, until just four cars from the front of the convoy, a driver : by himself indicated I would be ok for a lift with him. He shouted:

"Can you shoot?" ….. "Err …, yes, I can shoot".
…… "So, jump in, man.".

So, I did.

The Bounty Hunter

Sometimes you have experiences in life that, when you reflect on them, seem quite surreal. The white guy who was giving me a lift was called George. I struck up the usual conversation of course in response to his questions about where I was from, what I was doing there, where I had been, where I was going etc and so on. I was quite practiced at that by then as most people who gave me lifts often asked very similar questions. When I asked George what he did for a living, he replied :

"It's quite simple really; I just go out, kill terrorists
and get paid for it."

The convoy route from Musina to Bulawayo

What! Of course, I couldn't leave it at that could I? So, I followed up and asked him what that entailed, and he said he was a kind of "Bounty Hunter". He worked as a freelance mercenary for companies, or the wealthier farmers who owned large areas of land, and who wanted protection from terrorists. If he succeeded, he was paid an extra bonus of R\$1,000 for each dead terrorist and R\$500 per gun. So, I asked, "why do you do it?" and he said

> *"It's because I realised, I had an instinct for it*
> *when I was in the army. I'm good at tracking and*
> *hunting them down".*

What a crazy guy I thought. Just like on the way to Windhoek, George told me to open the glove compartment on my passenger side of the car and I saw there was a loaded army issue pistol stored in there. He said:-

> *"If any shit happens, that's your weapon. ....You*
> *know how to use it?".*

I explained I did from my two years as an Officer Cadet in the University Officer Training Corp. We'd done live fire weapons training and target practice with pistols just like that, as various rifles, SLR mainly, and machine guns, mainly Bren and Enfield Sten guns. He was quite pleased about that. At 1pm the officer in charge at the front gave the universal "move out" signal by holding his hand in the air and rotating it in a circular motion and everyone "mounted up" and started their engines so to speak. As the front Gun Ship set off, we all followed in convoy and rolled out from the outskirts of Beitbridge on our way to Bulawayo in the NW. I'm not sure of the speed, but everyone had to consistently maintain position and the same speed. It seemed quite slow moving at the time, probably 40mph, but might have been faster. Fortunately, we covered the miles without hitting a mine, being ambushed, or sniped at. There were no breakdowns either and we all arrived safely at about 5.40pm in Bulawayo. Even though there weren't any incidents along the way, every so often we passed burnt out vehicles pushed off onto the roadside and I could only imagine what tragedies had happened there. On George's recommendation I checked into the superb colonial elegance of the Selborne Hotel. It was named after Lord Selborne, High Commissioner of South Africa, who came to Bulawayo in 1906.

I'll just drive into a tree

I decided to spend the evening writing letters home and while I was doing that and looking out of the veranda of my bedroom onto the street below one of those strange things happened that continued the surreal theme of the whole day. A white bloke in a Morris Minor staggered into what I assume was his car. He looked supremely drunk. He then literally started it up and drove it straight into one of the big trees that ran down the side of the street. Fortunately, for him there was nobody else involved. Then the police arrived and took him away. The car was a write off, but he looked ok, but with that much to drink I suspect he would have spent the night locked up as a minimum before his court appearance. The next morning, I had a little time to explore the town before heading for the airport.

No Wheelchairs left?

I took the photo of a poor black person below, because I was rather staggered by his predicament:-

Poor disabled man in Bulawayo

He looked like he was crippled from the waist down and was unable to walk. Perhaps he had a spinal injury. He had "shoes" on both hands and was effectively "walking" using his arms by putting both in front and then swinging his whole body forward and down and then repeating the process. I felt sorry for him and wondered why nobody had managed to supply him with a wheelchair. That's what would have happened in the NHS in the UK.

Totally Bonkers

The following morning, the 22nd, I checked out of the hotel and caught the bus to Bulawayo Airport. The plane was probably a Vickers Viscount turbo prop plane which made up the bulk of the Air Rhodesia's planes at the time.

Air Rhodesia Vickers 748D Viscount at Bulawayo
(From Wikimedia Commons)

I must admit I was as aware, as almost everyone at the time was (it was big news), that two Air Rhodesia civilian airliners had been shot down by terrorists using Soviet heat seeking missiles in September 1978 and February 1979. So flying was a real risk, but then again, to be honest, that was part of the excitement – to experience a tiny piece of what it might be like to be in a war zone. I know…. totally bonkers. But then again when you are young, you think you are indestructible. According to the travel agent back in Musina it was a much safer option that taking the road. The flight took off at 10.30am and climbed high as soon as possible to get above the ceiling of shoulder-launched anti-aircraft missiles before heading NW at height for Victoria Falls.

During the in-flight service, Sonia, age about 20-21, who was one of the very pretty air hostesses on the plane, spent quite a bit of time chatting with me when she wasn't serving other passengers that was. I told her I was going to see the Falls and would be staying at the Victoria Falls Hotel. She popped back when she could to chat some more, and we got on well. So, towards the end of the flight, I plucked up the courage to ask if she would like to meet up one evening for a "date". I fully expected her to say "Thanks, but no thanks, I get asked that all the time", of course, especially from the various army types who were also on the plane. But hey, she said "yes", she would love to, and wrote down details of how to find where she was staying on a piece of paper. We arranged to go to see a film together on the night of the 24th when she would be staying over in Victoria Falls between flights.

Looking out of a washing machine window

When the plane arrived over Victoria Falls the pilots didn't do the usual gradual straight glide path stuff with a steady drop in height leading to a smooth landing. They tipped the plane virtually onto its wing tip, literally, and we began to spiral down rapidly towards the airport.

My window seat was on the side of the plane that was now facing the ground, so I could see the airport growing larger and larger below me as it revolved round and round below me out of my window. It was if I was looking out through a washing machine door window from the inside. I realised that that flight pattern kept the plane within a "cylinder column of space" above the airport and hopefully away from potential terrorists with Soviet ground to air missiles. Then, when we were low, he levelled the plane up rapidly, the horizon returned into sight, and we slid down in one smooth manoeuvre and landed. It was about 12.30pm. What a "rush" and quite a spectacular piece of flying.

As the plane sped down the runway decelerating fast, I could see a speeding armoured army vehicle on a road parallel to the runway about 150 yards away racing along at high speed trying the keep up with the plane. It was driving just this side of a high "POW camp style" tall, barbed wire fence. The vehicle had a manned heavy machine gun on the back pointing menacingly towards the bush beyond the fence. It was clearly there to take out any terrorists who decided to try and take a shot or two at the plane. A peek through the other side of the plane's windows revealed another identically armed vehicle speeding along doing the same on the other side of the runway. So, with our army escorts, the plane drew to a halt outside the main airport building and we disembarked. I had a final chat with Sonia and then jumped onto the shuttle bus for the Victoria Falls Hotel.

The Amazing Victoria Falls Hotel

The Victoria Falls Hotel was amazing. It's a beautiful Victorian structure that, to me, looked out of place in the middle of the bush and jungle. An alien spaceship dropped into the wrong place. What was most striking about it was its Victorian "British Empire" opulence, huge scale, with a palace style reception room, restaurant, long corridors, nicely decorated bedrooms, and incredible service. It's an experience I am so pleased to have had:

After checking in and settling into my room I went down to reception to make some enquiries and, taking their recommendation, I booked onto a guided tour scheduled for the following morning. Then I went out and spent some time wandering around the town. It wasn't very big, about the size of a village. So, there wasn't much to wander around. I wouldn't have minded a walk in the countryside around the town, but I'd been briefed at the hotel that there might be too many terrorists lurking about to do that safely and to stay within the perimeter fence. It reminded me of West Berlin, which at the time was surrounded and cut off by a wall, except in Victoria Falls it was built by the inhabitants. It was a beautiful day, so when I returned to the hotel I decided to just relax for a while. I put my trunks on, and sun bathed for a couple of hours by the swimming pool.

That evening I went to eat at a braii [BBQ] the hotel had put on which was lovely, then I went to the bar for a drink before meandering into the hotel casino. I just managed to stop myself from gambling. Instead, I watched all the other people losing lots of money, which was entertainment enough. The guests were all very ably entertained by Victoria Falls Hotel Glockenspiel Band playing on the hotel veranda:-

Victoria Falls Hotel Glockenspiel Band

The Sloshed Army Captain

Afterwards I went back and propped up the bar again when a Captain in the Zimbabwe-Rhodesian Army strolled in, dressed in his bush uniform, and ordered a double whisky which he downed and then another. We struck up a conversation. A girl called Lela, age mid 20s I'd say, also came up to the bar to buy a drink and happily joined into our conversation. The captain, his name was Ian, explained that he would be taking his platoon on patrol out beyond the perimeter security fence into the surrounding jungle and the bush around midnight into the early hours. At the start of the conversation, he'd asked me if I was in the Selou Scouts. I'd never heard of them, but he explained that they were a Special Forces unit in the Rhodesian Army that dressed less formally and many sported beards like mine. Hence, the question. Anyway, that cleared that up. All three of us had quite a few drinks before he went. I remember Lela asking him if he would be ok out on patrol after so many drinks. He said that "being sloshed" was the only way he could do it. It was bloody terrifying out there, pitch black most the time and you never knew whether you were going to come back unscathed, run into terrorists, get into a fire fight, and potentially get severally injured, or even end up in a body bag. Worst of all you might have to kill people. Then there was the potentially lethal wildlife to contend with too. Understandable. Anyway, his platoon sergeant appeared at the entrance to the bar and nodded.... That was the signal that it was time to head out, so with a thanks and a farewell to Lela and I, he went off, leaving us to continue in conversation. Well needless to say Lela and I were drunk

101

by the end of the night and what happened next is a little hazy.

Croc Farm

As I said earlier, on the 23rd I had booked myself onto a tour, so I dragged myself out of bed first thing and after breakfast I joined the rest of the tour group at the entrance to the hotel and off we went.

Our first stop was to my second crocodile farm where they bred and skinned them for bags, belts etc. It was just like the one I toured on the way back from St Lucia to Jo'burg. There were some cute ones and some bloody vicious big ones too. All quite interesting, but again rather sad. Good for the wild ones though and effectively the same treatment we dish out to sheep, cows and pigs isn't it?.

Here's a photo I took of the crocodile "farmer" showing us one of the babies in the Nursery, plus two of the enclosure where the mature breeding crocodiles were kept:-

Victoria Falls Crocodile Farm

David Livingstone and "The Big Tree",

Then we went to see "The Big Tree", where David Livingstone camped when he reached the Falls for the first time.

"The Big Tree" and David Livingstone's statue

He was a famous Christian missionary with the London Missionary Society, who explored Africa, and was one of the Victorian era's British celebrities. As well as trying to discover the sources of the Nile River, he named the falls after Queen Victoria in 1855. From there we went on to see Livingstone's statue which overlooks the Falls themselves.

The Falls

Then we went to the viewing areas to look at the Victoria Falls. They really are one of the Seven Wonders of the World. Just imagine a massive wall of water thundering down 500 feet. The force of the water was so great that spray went higher than the falls themselves and caused it to drizzle a mist of rain on the forest where we were stood. It wasn't a surprise then that the forest was tropical rain forest just like in the Tarzan movies. It was so different from the dried out bush not that far away. And it was the dry season too, so imagine what the falls would have been like in the wet season.

I hung back at the rear of the tour group so I could "steal" a bit of swing around on the jungle creepers just for fun. Just like Tarzan. When you are young you can do strange things. The Falls mark the border between Zambia (was called Northern Rhodesia pre-independence) and Zimbabwe-Rhodesia. So, the tour guide was careful where we went, and they warned us not to go too close to the viewpoints that were clearly visible from the Zambian side. If there were terrorist snipers there, they might take a pot shot.

Dry Bush and Leopard

After that, the tour bus took a safari drive through the Victoria Falls National Park. As I said, the area immediately around The Falls was tropical jungle supported by the almost continual humidity and spray generated by the Falls themselves. Not far from there though, the typical dry African bush predominated. We saw some wildlife on the safari including this leopard basking in the sun: I'd used a whole film during my last trip on safari on the way back from St Lucia, so I reserved only one shot for the leopard this time. The one on the left is the actual photograph and the one on the right is a blow up of the leopard from that:-

Leopard

Then the tour was over, and we were all returned to the hotel to disembark for the day.

Date Night

In the evening, if you recall, I'd previously arranged to take Sonia, the air hostess on the flight from Bulawayo, out to the cinema. I hadn't a clue what film was going to be on, but it was "21 Hours at Munich" about the massacre by the PLO of Jewish athletes at the Olympics in 1972. It was a pretty good film, but not the sort of movie to watch if you want to contain your imagination when you are wandering back to the hotel afterwards though town at night. Your imagination tells you there just might be a terrorist behind the many bushes bordering the path. I had a lovely time with Sonia, and I escorted her back to her staff house and bade her farewell in the customary fashion one does after a first (and only) date. There was another group of Zimbabwe-Rhodesian soldiers propping up the bar that night when I got back, so I had a chat with them over a few beers. Like the Captain the previous night they told me what it was like fighting the terrorists… "Sheer Hell". There was nothing romantic or heroic going on out there. It was a brutal conflict with little or no quarter given by either side. Lela was there too, and I think she thoroughly enjoyed being the centre of attention as an attractive and only female among a bunch of young red-blooded men.

Last Look at the Falls

On the morning of the 24th I rose as soon as possible at dawn and wandered down the Falls again for a final look before flying back from Victoria Falls to Bulawayo. There's a railway bridge by the Falls that connects the line between Zambia and Zimbabwe-Rhodesia. I'd assumed it would be closed due to international sanctions against Zimbabwe-Rhodesia, but it wasn't. I can say that for certain because a large diesel freight train, with many cargo wagons attached, moved slowly across the bridge from the Zambian side and rumbled away into the distance heading south through Victoria Falls Station. Quite a sight. I suppose it could have been Zambian exports heading down to South Africa for loading at Cape Town or Durban. I was rather surprised to see it though because I thought international sanctions had "cut" the line.

Dodging the missiles again

It just so happened that I was booked onto the same flight back as Lela. So, we checked in and sat together. Sonia wasn't on that flight. The plane rumbled down the runway escorted again by the armoured vehicles on either side, keeping up as best they could. The plane lifted off and spiralled back up to height as quickly as possible, before levelling and heading SE. We landed back in Bulawayo without incident. Lela had her car parked at the airport and she kindly gave me a lift into town. I shouldn't have stay with her for as long as I did though, because by that time, the armed escorted convoy to Beitbridge had already departed. Lela found out that the next one to the South African border was starting off from Essexvale first thing tomorrow morning at 7.30am.

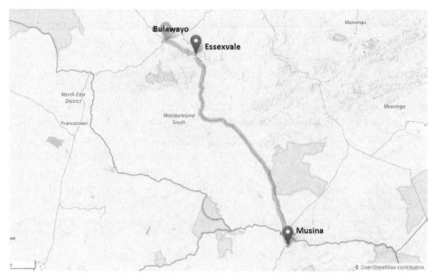

Bulawayo to Musina via Essexvale

Essexvale was on the road to the south east about 35 miles from Bulawayo. So, I had to decide. Risk it and try to get to Essexvale that evening or stay overnight in Bulawayo and try and hitch there at dawn. Tough one, but I decided to risk it and go that evening. I figured I needed to do that because I had arranged to meet Giles at lunchtime the following day in Beitbridge and to go to his friend's house for a braii over the border in the evening in Musina. As I've said already, there were no mobile phones back then, so there was no chance of a simple text message, video call, or DM in Twitter, or email. Or phone for that matter as Giles didn't have one where he was living either. You had to make plans.

Risking It

So, I made my farewells to Lela and started to hitch. You might be wondering why Lela couldn't give me a lift to Essexvale. Well, it was because I wouldn't let her. It was considered dangerous to travel without army escorts late in the afternoon and evening. She would be at work the following morning, so couldn't do that then either. With hindsight I should have realised that there would have been little or no traffic heading south to hitch a lift with anyway due to the lack of army protection. However, just when I was about to call it a day, accept that I'd made a big mistake and walk back into town and activate Lela's Plan B, a solitary farmer in a pickup truck came along, …….thumb out, big smile, eye contact , …..and he stopped.

Here's a Bag of Hand Grenades

He was heading to his farm just south of Essexvale, so he could drop me off, he said. I jumped in and he told me very deliberately, so I understood fully, that what we were doing was risky. He explained that he was going to floor the accelerator to drive at the fastest possible speed. Hopefully we would fly past any terrorists lurking in the bush waiting for sole travellers before they could even react. After asking me if I knew how to shoot, and I said "yes", explaining my limited, but just about adequate, army experience, he reached back and picked up a haversack full of hand grenades and passed them to me. He also gave me a loaded pistol. He said if any trouble kicked off, I had to get out of the vehicle fast, to throw myself in the ditch, or bush, by the roadside, keep very low and shoot anything that moved, except him, as well as throw the grenades at them. After pulling the pins of course, but I was to hug the ground after doing that as the shrapnel from them went all over the place. Anyway, he floored the accelerator, and we flew along the totally empty deserted highway to Essexvale at the highest speed he could get out of his vehicle, thankfully without incident. I couldn't see his speedo, but it felt like we were doing 100mph plus. As far as adrenalin rushes are concerned that trip was near the top. Was I frightened, yes, was it exciting, yes, very. An intoxicating combination. Was I staring keenly ahead and into the bush either side, looking for any indication of possible trouble? Dammed right I was.

He dropped me off and I booked into the Essexvale Hotel (not sure what I was going to do if the hotel was full with hindsight). It's since been renamed "The Why Not Hotel", and was looking a little run down and dilapidated from the outside in 2021. Essexvale is now called Esigodini.

Scotty, the Girls, and Special Branch

After settling into my room, I wandered over to the bar and spent the evening there. I met some crazy white Zimbabwe-Rhodesians, a black Zimbabwe-Rhodesian civil servant with another black guy who barely spoke and an alcoholic Scotsman in the Zimbabwe-Rhodesian Army, age about 55, called Scotty. He told me his "life story"….He and his wife had divorced, and he left Scotland and came to Rhodesia and joined the army 15 years ago. He couldn't find any other work. We drank together through the evening and could he drink!! He confessed that he was close to being an alcoholic, if not one already. My Scottish soldier friend briefly left the bar then came back about 10pm with a couple of pretty black girls, one for him and the other for me, he said with a big grin. He had paid for them both with his compliments. They were probably aged about 18-20 or so and they were very attractive but .... He wasn't too pleased when I politely thanked him and the girls and declined the opportunity, but after he realised I was not going to succumb to temptation, he left with both girls. I'm sure he had a great time with them although how he was going to manage after drinking so much, I'm not quite sure. Why did I decline his offer? They were very pretty, lovely smiles and were clearly quite relaxed at the "task" ahead of them, no doubt lubricated by the money. There was a genuineness about them that suggested that what they were doing was perfectly normal to them. It would have been an "interesting" experience I must admit and one that sorely tempted me, but it was just that I had never paid before and didn't feel like I wanted to start then. It was a bit like the girls in the Kalahari Sands Hotel night club in Windhoek. I felt the same way then. They were apparently there for that purpose as well as dancing, but I just couldn't do it. I think the moral code I had been taught during my Christian upbringing still had a brake on at least some of my moral inhibitions.

After my Scottish soldier friend went off with the girls, I remained sitting at the bar when I was engaged in conversation by the black "civil servant" called Joseph, or Joe as he liked to be called. He had also been in there for some time and had watched the "girl episode" too, which he clearly thought was a good source of much laughter and amusement. I tried to explain my "position", but he couldn't grasp why I had declined. Were they not beautiful? I would have had a great time with them, wouldn't I? ......and so on. . He'd had quite a few drinks too, so he was "well lubricated" and perhaps spoke more freely than he might otherwise to my questions about where he was from, what he did and so on. He said that he at first thought I worked for the South African secret police, because I kept slipping in the odd Afrikaner word like "danki" (thanks). Joseph assumed that was a slip up on my part, but I assured him it was only that I had picked up some of the local lingo during my travels. There was another black guy with him who was already very drunk and beyond rationale conversation and eventually passed out in his seat. When I asked Joe what his friend did for a living, he said he "worked for the Special Branch and did anything nasty that needed doing". He seemed quite decent when he was drunk before he passed out.

Joe went on, with my encouragement, to explain what the Special Branch did and his views on the ZANU-ZAPU-Rhodesian Bush War. He was quite perceptive I think and what he said was a complete revelation to me, much of which turned out to be true. So, he said that not all "black people" in Zimbabwe-Rhodesia were of the same political persuasion, identity, or cultural background. There were broadly two tribes, Matabele here in the west and Shona in the east. The Matabele terrorists usually joined ZAPU [Zimbabwe African People's Union] and the Shona, ZANU [Zimbabwe African National Union]. Those were the two terrorist organisations fighting the government in the Bush War and both adhered to a communist ideology, not western democratic capitalism. The "British" (the white Rhodesians) had maintained a peace between the tribes. It was also a proxy Cold War. ZAPU were being supplied by Russia and ZANU by China he said. Just like the Afrikaner I talked to during my journey to Cape Town. Similarly, he said that, as tribes, they had identities that were as different as, say, English and French.

He was a Matabele and so was his Special Branch friend. The problem was that neither the Matabele nor Shona would be happy to be ruled by the other he said. Shona occupied about two thirds of the country in the east and made up about three quarters of the black population and Matabele the rest in the west. So, the Matabele were outnumbered. The Shona would inevitably have a majority of seats in government when "one man, one vote" came in. He dreaded that, because there was then probably going to be a very bloody civil war where the Shona would massively outnumber the Matabele. That's why he was working on the government side.

I did some research in 2021 and it turns out he was spot on. Following independence Shona ZAPU became the governing party and the Matabele ZANU and Matabele population generally suffered many atrocities in the 1980s, especially at the hands of government's 5th Brigade. When I investigated this further, I discovered that that period has since been recognised internationally as racially motivated genocide by Shona on Matabele. Also, I have since found out that the "Special Branch" was a highly effective Rhodesian government counter insurgency force made up of whites and blacks. They employed rather ruthless tactics to basically track down and kill terrorists in the Bush War and they were very good at it. So, they could be viewed as being closer in function to the SAS than a police force.

Quite an evening really. Anyway, we all eventually called it a night. By the end of the evening (midnight) I was drunk and so was he. We got on well though and we all left the bar amicably. He basically hauled his Special Branch friend out. I suspect he wasn't a "civil servant" though looking back. He was probably Special Branch too. Even so, the conversation had made me feel a little unsettled. However, I basically crashed out and fell asleep. Thankfully all went well overnight, and I awoke alive and hung over the following morning on the 25th. I was still up for breakfast first thing though. How I managed to get up amazes me. I had the constitution of an ox in those days. After checking out I stepped out to walk the queue of cars lining up for the convoy to hitch a lift on the 7:30am armed convoy from Essexville to Beitbridge.

The convoy was escorted by the army with the same type of armoured "crocodile" vehicles as on the way up. The mounted machine guns pointed into the bush on either side and, if anyone attacked, they would be met with a withering hail of bullets. A chap in a lovely big 1960's Humber Snipe offered me a lift with his wife and two children. They were on their way to South Africa they said. What a car. Really nice. They were keen to listen to the stories of my travels and the journey passed quickly. Fortunately, there were no terrorist incidents along the way. The convoy covered the same route back that I had went up on without being ambushed or sniped at and everyone arrived safely in Beitbridge at the border. I met up with Giles as planned and we returned over the border and back to Musina by 12 noon.

On arrival I had a bite to eat then wrote letters home. I met up with Giles again at 3pm. Giles and I had been invited to a braii (BBQ) at his friend's Babs and Wolfies's house in the evening (originally from Germany I think). They were very nice and made me so welcome. They had asked me to come along before I set off from Musina to go to the Falls. Everyone had a great time chatting. I had some steak and quite a few beers and dropped into bed about 11:45pm. I'm not sure whose place it was, but someone let me stay in their little house down the bottom of the garden. That would be where a servant would have lived, I guess. It was small, but comfortable and I had one of the best night's sleep ever. The following morning, I remember waking up on the 26th at 9am thinking what a comfortable sleep I had had, but I was still feeling groggy from the beer the nights before. So, I had an extra sleep in.

Later that day I met up with Giles and we went back over the border to Beitbridge for braii at Peter's Motel. For some reason I don't recall, Giles bought some champagne on the way to give to the host. Perhaps it was a birthday party, or similar anniversary? The braii was excellent and, to me, free. While I was there I picked up a little of the history of "Peter's Motel". It was named after Peter Dahl who set it up in the 1960s; there was another place he owned too at Victoria Falls. Giles first met him when he went down to Beitbridge. They were great plane enthusiasts apparently. Peter had one of two Beechcraft Staggerwing aircraft in Africa. He famously flew it underneath Beitbridge's bridge where it crossed the Limpopo and clipped the sand with the brand new propeller and had to order another one.

Currency Smuggling

As we approached the border crossing to go back to South Africa, I still had some Rhodesian currency notes on me. I asked Giles about it. I had not thought about it before when I had crossed back the previous day, but Giles said it was illegal to take Rhodesian currency out of the country. We were already in the border queue, so I folded the notes up and put them down my sock. By doing so I effectively became a currency smuggler. I recall being a little nervous going through customs, but they did nothing and just waved us through. I guess Giles was a very well-known person on the border given that he was to and fro all the time. That probably gave me a little "protection". I ended up giving it to Giles on the other side anyway in exchange for the equivalent in Rands. With hindsight I should have told Giles earlier and done that on the Rhodesian side first, but there you go. Later that evening Giles and I went to his friend's Sebastian's house to just relax, chat, and watch TV.

Back to Jo'burg

On the 27th, Giles's friend, a girl he called "Tossy", gave me a lift to Pietersburg (now renamed Polokwane) about half way to Jo'burg Obviously "Tossy" wasn't her real name, and I had no idea what that was, or why Giles called her "Tossy".

Source: OpenStreetMap

She was great company and the tine passed very quickly. She kindly dropped me off at a good hitch hiking spot on the Jo'burg facing side of town, wished me luck, and sped off to her meeting. Then I thanked her for the lift and set off to hitch from there to Johannesburg.

Black Political Activists

I was eventually offered a lift by three 3 black guys, in about their mid-twenties. I must admit when they pulled up, I did have an uneasy feeling and I seriously thought about declining the lift. Come to think of it, apart from those that wanted paying for the lift near Windhoek and the black co-driver in the sheep truck on the way to Cape Town, they were the first black people I'd shared a lift with. The strange thing was that the front passenger got out and offered me the seat in front and he got in the back with the other guy. So, I took a risk, got in and off we went. I must admit I was a bit worried I was in trouble when I asked them what they were doing they told me they were "political activists" on their way to a meeting. It instantly crossed my mind, does that extend into terrorist territory and am I about to become a casualty? I was initially worried that I might to get a bullet in the back of the head, or a rope round my neck. On the other hand, having a white guy clearly visible in the front passenger seat could be a smart move for them. Anyway, the driver wound down the window and was very friendly as he asked me where I was heading and the others were smiling too. I had to make a snap decision and my darker thoughts were overridden by their friendliness, so I decided yes, it's a genuine lift offer. My head said this could also be a very welcome and rare opportunity to get to learn more of their perspectives. They were keen to know more about me, so they quizzed me about life in the UK and my travels around and impressions of southern Africa. That was fine, things relaxed a lot, and we had a good chat. I then quizzed them about their stories. They had all felt they had a good education and had decided to have a career as politically active campaigners. They belonged to the part of the party that wanted to effect democratic change from within, not the "armed struggle" part. They said they believed that one day there would be a full democracy in place where everyone had a vote. They hoped that everyone would be able to live together, no matter which tribal, colour or racial background they had. That had to be one of the most uplifting and encouraging conversations I had had during the whole trip. I was glad I had accepted the lift, or that opportunity would not have presented itself. Their views very much echoed those of Nelson Mandela that saved South Africa, in my opinion, from what could have become a very bloody civil war.

6,060 miles so far

They dropped me at their turnoff about half way to Jo'burg. It was a couple of lifts later when I eventually got back to Jo'burg and The Little House. It was great to see Jenny and David again and we spent the evening chatting about my adventures. I'd covered a total of another 1,375 miles going to Victoria Falls and back. When I added the 4,685 miles I had covered before that I'd covered 6,060 miles so far.

So, I thought having the 28th as a bit of a rest day was fine by me. A chance to relax, digest, reflect and writing letters home, I also went to the bank and arranged £90 in travellers' cheques for my return trip to the UK. Then I met Jenny for lunch at the Wimpy Bar, who had popped out of work to meet me. After that I made my way back to their place in the Bez Valley and cooked everyone a beef curry for tea. A very pleasant evening was spent chatting, eating curry, and drinking.

On the 29th I went back to Barclays for the travellers' cheques. Then I had lunch with Jenny again in the Wimpy Bar. After that I went to the Afrikaner Museum (now renamed Museum Africa) for a couple of hours. At that time, it mainly displayed the history of southern Africa from the Dutch and British settlers' perspective. After that I went back to The Little House and wrote to Anastasia. She had written and invited me to go straight from Heathrow when I flew in from South Africa to stay with her in The Hague in Holland. She said I could stay as long as I liked, so, as I had a week free on return, I decided that was an opportunity not to be missed. I wrote back to her to accept her invitation. In the days before the internet, I had no idea how I was going to get to The Hague, but figured out I would find a way. More on that adventure in another story.

13. THE GOLDEN MILE BECKONS

Off to Durban

Pondering my little map of South Africa and retracing my routes so far, I had decided I just had to fill the obvious gap in my adventures with a trip to Natal and its capital, Durban, then on through Transkei and the small independent mountainous kingdom of Lesotho, before returning to Jo'burg. I'd read about Durban, the beautiful coastal capital city of Natal, its nightlife and its "Golden Mile" beaches. I'd acquired a taste for the warmer climate from my visit to St Lucia. Durban was named after Lieutenant Governor D'Urban of Cape Province, and their city hall was the same design as the one in Belfast, Northern Ireland. The beckoning mountain scenery in Lesotho was meant to be spectacular too. So, no sooner was I back from Victoria Falls than I was off again the next day. Jenny and David were still in work of course full time, so I couldn't expect them to entertain and look after me.

At 7am on the 30th I was all set waiting for the arrival of one of the friends I'd made in Jo'burg called Arthur. He had offered the previous day to help kick off my next trip with a lift to a good jumping off point on the outskirts. He arrived promptly, so I said my farewells and thanks to Jenny and David and off we went. He was a lovely guy and a very thoughtful "Grandfather type" figure. I think he was a little concerned for my safety from the conversation during the short journey. He was right to be of course, but when you are young and less experienced in the ways of the world your conception of risk can be different. So, having failed to persuade me otherwise about the risks of hitch hiking, he dropped me off at an ideal hitch-hiking spot on the southern outskirts of Jo'burg.

114

Liverpudlian Ex-Policeman

Picking good hitch hiking spots was something I had considerable experience of by now. You needed good visibility for vehicles coming towards you and a place off the side of the road just after where you were standing so they could easily, and safely pull in. Entrance ramps to main highways and the exists of roundabouts were also good because the vehicles were going slow. I was very lucky to not have to wait long at all. My lift was from a guy, probably in his 50's, called Teddy. I could tell immediately from his accent that he was a Liverpudlian from England. Turns out he was an ex-policeman who had become a very rich businessman since he emigrated to South Africa. He insisted on buying me lunch on the way which was very good of him.

One notable observation about hitch hiking was that it taught me to be a hell of a lot more observant of human personalities, who was probably "safe", who might not be "so safe" and therefore when to accept a lift offer, or decline. In this case buying me lunch was just buying me lunch and nothing more. Here's the route I took:-

Jo'burg to Durban in Natal

"Young man, there's a place you can go...."

I booked into the YMCA just like in Cape Town, and in the famous song by Village People, it was cheap, but good quality. It only cost the equivalent of R5.50 (about £3) per day for bed, breakfast, lunch, and dinner. That included my own single room too, not in a dormitory. That's the equivalent of about £15 in 2021. Durban was a beautiful place . There was a long beach, waves that towered above me and lots of sunshine. I spent that evening walking along the "The Golden Mile". beach front taking in the atmosphere. The sand was soft, and the seawater wasn't cold either. There were bars, many of them, dotted all along the beachfront buildings. It reminded me a little of Blackpool, but was more up market. I took a photo from my room at the YMCA looking across the road towards the sea and the Durban Point port area:-

View across Durban's bay from the YMCA.

If you know Durban now, you might be thinking "that's not where the YMCA is", but back in 1979 it was there, on the beach front. It moved later, further away from the beach front. I discovered that when I was writing this.

"Reserved for the White Race"

The following day on the 31st August the weather was lovely, so I just spent the day on the beach sunbathing and swimming, pretty much what everyone else on the beach was doing. Here's a couple of photos I took:-

Durban beach

Like several of my photos they had suffered a bit from being in storage in the intervening years from 1979. It was good to scan them though, before they became more degraded.

Bathers typically waded out into the sea close to where the waves were breaking then they "body surfed" back in again on the gigantic waves that rolled in constantly from the vast Indian Ocean. There weren't any bathers with surf boards which was a bit unexpected. Everyone didn't seem a bit concerned about the possibility of sharks lurking out there looking for a quick snack, which I recalled from my earlier trip to St Lucia. I also noticed, as the day wore on, that I was getting a suntan without burning. It's worth pointing out though that there were no people swimming there who were not white. In fact, they were not allowed to at that point in time, because apartheid was still very much alive and enforced by signs on the beach front that said. Here's the words on the sign which were repeated in Afrikaans and Zulu:-:-

---

"CITY / STAD DURBAN"

"UNDER SECTION 37 OF THE DURBAN BEACH BY-LAWS, THIS BATHING AREA IS RESERVED FOR THE SOLE USE OF MEMBERS OF THE WHITE RACE GROUP"

HIERDIE GEBIED IS, INGEVOLCE ARTIKEL 37 VAN DIE DURBANSE STRANDVERORDENINCE, UITGEHOU VIR DIE UITSLUITLIKE GEBBRUIK VAN LEDE VAN DIE BLANKE RASSEGROEP.

NCAPHANSI KWESICABA 37 SOMTHETHO WAMAB HISHI ASETHEKWINI. LENDAWO IGCINELWE UKUSETSHENZISWA NGAMALUNGU OHLANGA OLUMHLOPHE JUPHELA.

Here's my translations : -

Afrikaans into English:

THIS AREA, IN ACCORDANCE WITH ARTICLE 37 OF THE DURBAN BEACH REGULATIONS, IS RESERVED FOR THE EXCLUSIVE USE OF MEMBERS OF THE WHITE RACE GROUP.

Zulu into English

**UNDER SECTION 37 OF THE EARTHLY BUSINESS ACT. THIS SITE IS
RESERVED FOR USE BY MEMBERS OF THE WHITE RACE ONLY**

Signs like that have since been relegated to museums. or the scrap yard to be dumped or recycled.

Unfortunately, about 3:30pm, some thunder clouds rolled in from the ocean at such a speed that it seemed like, at one minute, it was beautiful sunshine, and the next it was pouring down, albeit not for long. So, after sheltering till the worst was over, I abandoned the beach and went into Durban for a look around the city, passing the stunning town hall. While I was wandering around the city avoiding most of the rain, I spotted a second-hand book stall, so I picked out three. One was about the private life of King Charles II of Great Britain and Ireland (1660–85). The second one about Warsaw in World War II. The third one was about the pioneers of surgery in 18th Century London. With the other book I am reading, on President Nixon and the Watergate scandal in the USA, I had plenty to keep me occupied in the quieter moments, although when exactly they would be I wasn't sure. Still the long flight home could give me some time to read.

Having a Blitz in The London Town Pub

I met a guy at the YMCA called Graeme, mid 20s, who worked for an advertising agency in Durban. On the Friday evening he and his friends were going out to a place called The London Town Pub,. When I looked it up recently it looks like it was part of the Claridges Hotel, but had unfortunately closed. Previous social media comments described it as a popular, loud, wet T shirt, yard of ale competition type, raucous nightspot. That was pretty accurate. They asked me to come along, so I said yes. I have to say that night out was one of the most enjoyable evenings I have ever had. It was such a surreal experience.

I'll try and describe the place. It was large bar room with a high ceiling and the place was kitted out with loads of World War 2 and London memorabilia, numerous posters, like the "Keep Calm and Carry On" type poster plus many copies of old photos and so on. There were rows of tables and pews and a real full size red double decker London Bus, literally, inside the pub. That provided additional seating and atmosphere, plus a red British telephone box. The ambiance of the place was added to by the playing of well-known WW2 songs over the PA system while films of the London Blitz and Winston Churchill speeches projected onto a big cinema type screen. Having been given song sheets on the way in many of the happy frolickers joined in renditions of the songs. My memories are a little "Castle lagered" but I'm guessing that could have included "It's a long way to Tipperary", "There'll be Bluebirds over the White Cliffs of Dover", and "Pack up your troubles in your old kit bag", and so on. The singing volume and joviality grew as the evening went on and the quantity of beer consumed increased. Like everyone, I had a thoroughly enjoyable time, before staggering back to the YMCA with Graeme and friends, who thankfully knew where it was. I hadn't a clue. I happily bade my goodnights, hit the sack and crashed out for the night.

The following day, Saturday, 1st September, was a "day after the night before event", one for recovery and recreation. So, I headed for The Golden Mile beach and sunbathed and swam there until about 3pm when the rain came on suddenly again. So, well on the way to recovery, I wandered back to the YMCA where I spent the evening watching TV and chatting with the other residents in the communal lounge. I seemed to be about the only one there who was passing "through" on holiday. All the others were using it as a home from home, mainly as students, or young people working in Durban whose family lived too far out for them to commute I and out daily. It was great to chat with them. After that I caught up with writing and letters home.

On The Beach and a Radio Commercial"

It was raining and cloudy on Sunday, the 2nd, so I had a walk around town again and then, once the rain ceased, along the beach front too. I regressed into childhood a little going for dodgem rides in the Durban's Marine Parade Amusement Park on the beachfront [which had been renamed to "Durban Funworld"]. I had a look around Fitzsimmons Snake "Zoo" which contained exhibits of hundreds of different types of live snakes (it closed down in 2008 apparently to make way for "a redevelopment").

Afterwards I went for a stroll along Snake Park Beach:. Later on, that day, back at the YMCA, I wrote another letter home, then went for a drink at a local bar before returning to the YMCA in the evening to find they were going to show a film called "Meat Balls". So, I decided to watch it with other residents. It was a comedy about USA Youth Camp.

The following day on Monday, the 3rd September, I went to look around Durban Museum in the morning. The afternoon was spent hanging out and chatting with two guys I met, Graeme and Derek (a Rhodesian). In the evening we went to the cinema to see Rocky 2, which I thought was an "excellent film"….. at the time.

I spent the morning on Tuesday the 4th sunbathing on the beach and writing while I was there. I wrote that I really liked it in Durban, the YMCA was cheap, their sunshine was permanent, well until mid-afternoon anyway, and there was a beautiful beach on which to do a lot of nothing all day. Graeme had asked me if I would like to see how his advertising agency made commercials for the radio. I obviously said "yes", so off we went to the recording studio in the afternoon. There were three actors in a soundproof room who recited the words of the script through several takes which were recorded, while Graeme directed the process. I sat in the recording booth and watched. It was really fascinating. Afterwards a successful recording was completed he had to go back to his office to work. So I went to the beach, although by that time it was getting close to teatime and most sun bathers had gone home. Still for me it was like an English summer climate, while for them, it was winter.

More Beach and Tavern

On Wednesday the 5th I spent the day on the beach again. The weather was beautiful, so I went in for a few swims too. Later that evening I went along to a pub called "The Tavern". While I was propping up the bar, one of the other residents at the YMCA spotted me and came over to say "hi". She was called Amanda and she pulled me into her group of friends, because she thought "I looked lonely". Very nice of her. They wanted to know all about my travels around southern Africa and Zimbabwe-Rhodesia. Amanda's parents lived in the country in the northwest of Natal. She was studying in Durban and living in the week at the YMCA. It was really good value, so that's why she, and many other students, lived there. I had a really great time chatting together with them, then we wandered back to the YMCA after closing time.

On Thursday the 6th during the day I spent my time relaxing and sunbathing on the beach. The weather was beautiful. I fell asleep a few times then I went to see a film called "Prophesy" in the early evening. It wasn't very good at all. Afterwards I sat in the communal lounge reading the papers. I saw Amanda returning to the YMCA and she spotted me, so wandered over. After chatting for a while and getting on well, we decided to go out for a few drinks at The Tavern pub again.

Amanda versus Lesotho

My original plan was to leave Durban on Friday the 7th and embark on another adventure trip south west along the coast of Natal and swing right into the mountains and explore Lesotho. Having met Amanda though, I changed my mind and extended my stay over the weekend to the Monday. I know …lost opportunity.. but she was rather lovely. So, in the day, as the weather wasn't too good, I took the opportunity to visit the Durban Museum again, Art Gallery and the Natal History Museum while she was studying, then we met up again in the evening and went out together into town.

On the 8th, Saturday, Amanda and I spent the day together relaxing on the beach. then we went for a quick drink at The Tavern before returning to the YMCA and chatting till very late. On Sunday the 9th, Amanda and I went sun bathing and swimming on Durban beach all morning and afternoon again. Then we spent the evening together at the YMCA lounge watching TV with Graeme, Derek and others. I would be setting off tomorrow to go back to Johannesburg, so it was a kind of "leaving do" for me.

So, on Monday September 10th I said my sad farewells to Amanda and, after breakfast, I started to hitch back to Jo'burg. I made for the edge of the city and started hitching a lift and, by 10am, I was on my way and arrived back just after 10pm. Out of those, 8 hours was spent in various lifts and 4 hours was spent at various points waiting at the road side. I had two memorable lifts.

The first was with a young lady who was driving back to her family's farm from Durban. The interesting thing about her was her dialect and the way that she spoke. It was just the same as the girl at The Forrester Arms in Swaziland. Probably the best way to describe it was that her accent as upper middle, or upper class "home counties". That's not a criticism of her, by the way, as she was great fun and full of laughter and we got on well. I had to ask, and she said that her accent was typical of English descendants in Natal. Apparently, Natal voted in favour of staying as a Dominion when South Africa held a vote on whether to become a republic in 1960. The vote overall was narrow with 52% in favour of a republic. Unfortunately, all things come to an end and the turn off for her parent's place came up and I had to say farewell, get out and start hitching again.

Zulu with Two Wives

The longest, and really interesting, lift, was from the edge of Natal all the way back to Jo'burg with a black Zulu businessman from Natal. He was probably aged about 45 to 50 and was a well-built, large, stocky person. That was quite a long journey, so we had loads of time to talk. He told me he was an ex-smuggler in his youth. He was on his way from his home in Natal to his other home in Soweto. He had a wife and children in Natal and another wife and children in Soweto. He explained that having two families was expensive, but it was a custom among Zulus that a man could have more than one wife. Although in law he only had one legal wife, under Zulu custom he was married to both. I took the opportunity to chat with him about the apartheid question to see what he had to say.

So, he said it was a mistake to think of them, the black population, as one group, because there were many different tribes in South Africa. Tribal allegiance was strong, and their tribal structures were hierarchical with the head man, or the chief, at the top. In Soweto there were frequent and bloody fights between Zulus and other tribes which he called "Bantus".

Having the "whites" in charge provided stability. As a businessman he liked "stability". It was good for profits. He feared that if hostilities escalated out of control it could be a blood bath, not just of whites against blacks and vice versa, but blacks against blacks, as different tribes vied for power. Other interesting points he made was that giving "tribute" to "the chief" was normal and respectful, or to someone in a position of power, such as a government official, in exchange for favours or requests. We would normally call that "corruption". Zulu wealth was traditionally measured by the number of cattle a man had too he said, but that wasn't good, because it could lead to overgrazing.

Stranded on the edge of Jo'burg

As I said, it was a long journey, and he was going to Soweto. It was dark by the time we reached the outskirts of Jo'burg and he pulled onto the side of the road on the southern edge of the city to drop me off. He said that was the closest point to Bez Valley to the north. Soweto, which was where he was going on the western side of Jo'burg was not somewhere I wanted to be at night, he said. So I thanked him for the lift, he wished me well and then drove off. I guessed there was roughly about 10 miles of Jo'burg suburbs from that point to Bez Valley where Jenny and David lived. It felt unsafe to be honest in the dark, so I began walking north towards Bez Valley as quickly as possible, thinking I'd catch a taxi, or jump on a bus if I saw one. Then I came across a phone box. So, I called their house. They were already in bed, so I woke them up and were surprised to hear from me so late. I explained my predicament and they were clearly very concerned for my safety. So, they asked me to tell them the intersection street names at the nearest corner of where I was. Of course, it was dark, so I had to let the phone dangle while I rushed to the corner to read the street names, then dash back. Fortunately, my supply of coins didn't run out. Thankfully they were able to drive out arriving about 20 minutes later and I was back at theirs safe and sound shortly afterwards. That must have come as a surprise to them. Me turning up like that. It was nice to read letters from home which were waiting for me.

The following day on the 11th I spent relaxing, sunbathing, and generally doing nothing except reading my books and, later, I played chess with David. Also, a letter arrived from Anastasia that she had written to me while she was on holiday with her parents in southern France reiterating that I was invited to go there to see her in Holland after returning from South Africa. I wrote back confirming that I would and setting broad details of when that was likely to be.

14. PRETORIA

Voortrekker Monument, Pretoria

There was one major gap still in my touring plan and that was Pretoria. I wanted to see the sights. After all it was the capital of South Africa. So, the next day on the 12th September I took the rather modern train to Pretoria. My first stop was the Voortrekker Monument, a massive granite structure located on a hilltop just to the south of Pretoria. My interest in it was first generated by the Afrikaner who tried his best to improve my knowledge of his cultural history way back on my first journey to Cape Town. It was built to commemorate the Afrikaner Voortrekkers exit out of Cape Colony in their wagons on "the Great Trek" between 1835 and 1854 to escape British rule. They established the Orange Free State and Transvaal.

What was clear from its scale and design was that the trek had deep cultural, ideological, and symbolic significance to Afrikaners. It reminded me of the Rhodes Memorial in Cape Town. The huge monument was located on a hill overlooking the city. Here a couple of the photos I took:-

Voortrekker Monument and view towards the city.

One thing that struck me during the visit was the signs that underscored the apartheid system. Non-whites were only allowed access on Tuesday mornings:-

Sign on left:

VOORTREKKER MONUMENT
RIGHT OF ADMISSION RESERVED
VISITING HOURS: WHITES DAILY (EXCEPT TUEDAYS) INCLUDING
PUBLIC HOLIDAYS 09h00 TO 16h45
SUNDAYS 14h00 TO 16h45
NON-WHITES TUESDAYS 08h30 to 12h00
CLOSED ON CHRISTMAS DAY AND GOOD FRIDAY
BY ORDER, BOARD OF CONTROL

Sign on right:
VOORTREKKER MONUMENT, PRETORIA
(RIGHT OF ADMISSION RESERVED)

1.   **VISITORS MUST PLEASE BE SUITABLY DRESSED eg. ADULTS WITH BARE FEET, LADIES IN SHORTS (TIGHTS) OR MEN IN SLEEVELESS SHIRTS ARE NOT ALLOWED.**
2.   **NO ANIMALS**
3.   **NO FOOD eg. ICE CREAM, SWEETS ETC.**

BY ORDER, BOARD OF CONTROL

Union Building

After completing my visit to the monument, I went over to see the very impressive Union Building in Pretoria. That's the seat of government and office of the President as well. The Parliament met in Cape Town at that time. I took the photo looking from the main veranda of the building towards the city centre:-

Government Building

After that I went for a walk around the city centre before heading back to Jo'burg by train and met Jenny and David, plus many friends, at the PiG in the evening. We had yet another excellent lager filled evening.

15. END OF DAYS

The Last Stand

It was the 13th September and I only had three more days left before my flight back to the UK. Arthur and Iris dropped by The Little House to catch up on my travel news, then invited me along for a visit to the plot of land where they were building their new retirement house, or their "stand" as they called it. They hoped their builder would complete the work some time in 1980. That was a normal approach in South Africa apparently. You bought a plot of land in an area designated as "residential", then had a house built to your own design.

Dinner at Julia's

Then in the evening I took up an invite from Julia to pop round to her apartment in the trendy district of Hillbrow to see her again. She'd prepared a lovely meal too and we had a very enjoyable evening together. She was very keen to learn all about my travels since we'd last met. We also discussed the "incident" of me being "caught" in her bath by her Jo'burg boyfriend when he turned up unexpectedly and things became a little tense. We had a good laugh about that with hindsight, although it wasn't funny at the time it happened. Ample excellent South African red wine probably helped and she told me all about being in love with two guys, one in Jo'burg and another in Cape Town, and she was finding it very difficult, impossible in fact. to choose between them. It was a real dilemma for her which she probably wasn't going to be resolving any time soon she thought. Julia wrote to me afterwards a couple of times just after I arrived back in the UK. Her last letter ended with "I think about you every day, cuddles, hugs and kisses, Julia xxxx". After that our correspondence ended. Why? I don't know. She just didn't reply to my letters anymore. That always intrigued me.

What happened to her? Giles knew Julia too. I asked him about her recently when I stumbled across his contact details online. The last time he saw her was in 1981 and she was very pregnant he said. I wonder if she did choose one of them in the end?

Farewells, Packing and Take off

On the 14th I nursed a hangover courtesy of a late night and ample wine at Julia's, so spent the day relaxing and not doing much except thinking about my adventures and last night. I had a lot to take in, write up and digest. Then on the 15th I packed all my things and a few souvenirs, which didn't take long as I hadn't got all that much to pack, and then relaxed. I still managed to leave behind a jacket, trousers, and jumper though that were in the wash basket.

Finally, the dreaded 16th arrived, and it was nearly all over. I played squash with David as usual (I don't recall who won}, then some of the people I'd met in Jo'burg were invited round by Jenny and David to The Little House for my "leaving do" braii and to wish me well before I left. We had a very pleasant time sitting in the garden just chatting and relaxing.

Just a note on a few souvenirs which I picked up along the way and still have. Here is a recent photo of them: -

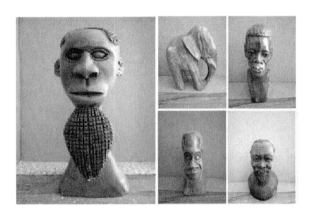

The one on the left is 9 inches high and carved from hard wood. Apart from the bottom right bearded man sculpted from clay, all the rest, the elephant, and the two other heads are sculpted from soap stone. All are made skillfully by South Africans and acquired by me from roadside stalls and local shops during my travels.

To the Airport

On 16th September after saying goodbye to Jenny and David and thanking them for a superb stay and their incredible generosity as well as putting up with me for such a long time, they drove me to Jan Smuts Airport. At 4.45pm I went through check in and boarded without a ny problem and my flight for London [SA234] took off 30 minutes later than scheduled at 6:30pm. The flight back went smoothly. I was seated beside a lady who said she was a Lord's daughter [age about 55], who was nice to chat to. She had her South African maid with her who was a "Cape Coloured". She was going to meet relatives related to her white grandfather's Scottish ancestors who lived in Edinburgh, Scotland. That was interesting. Apparently inter-racial marriage did happen frequently many years ago, such as between British soldiers posted out there who decided to stay on and settle. She said she was descended from one such relationship. The really sad thing was that as a "Cape Coloured" she was classified as "non-white", which meant her movements, and where she could live, were restricted significantly under the apartheid system. The flight went off without any hitches and I arrived at Heathrow Airport, London, just over 13 hours later at 8:05am on Monday 17th September.

From London to Holland

As I said earlier, Anastasia had written to me and invited me to stay on my return. So, after I'd collected my luggage and passed through Immigration and Customs, I telephoned her in Holland. That involved acquiring a pile of coins and feeding them into a phone in a public phone box. There were no mobile phones in those days and international calls were expensive. So, the conversation was not long and had to be to the point, as was the case with most phone conversations in those days due to the cost. There were no free minute monthly allowance bundles then. She was delighted to hear from me and confirmed that the offer to come and see her in The Hague still stood. I had broadly figured out how to get there and a likely timetable. I said I hoped to see her at The Hague railway station at about 10:30pm that evening.

First, I caught the train and tube trains from Heathrow to London's Charring Cross Station and then the 11:28am to Dover. The best available option over the English Channel was by hovercraft to France. So, I bought a ticket on that. It was fast and took only 45 minutes. Then I caught a train to Lille, another train to Brussels, and from there onto the final train to The Hague. Everything ran to schedule, so I met Anastasia at the railway station at exactly 10:30pm as planned. It was quite some journey and that, my friends, is where this part of the story almost ends.

16. LOOKING BACK

How many miles?

Before I went to Durban, I had toured for about 6,060 miles. Adding on the 710 miles for the Durban round trip, pushed that up to 6,770 miles. Adding in the 90 miles for the trip to Pretoria, that's 6,860. If you add some more miles for touring within each of the destinations I stayed at, say another 700 miles at an average of 10 miles a day over 10 weeks, that pushes the estimated total mileage to about 7,560 for the southern African tours.

Adding in the 390 miles from Heathrow to The Hague, about 400 miles touring around Holland, and the 720 miles from The Hague back to North West England pushes the grand total for the whole time to about 9,070 miles in total.

If the 320 miles from Preston station to Heathrow and 11,200 miles for the return flight to Johannesburg are added, that makes the start to end grand total 20,590 miles.

"Having your cake and eating it"

I noted in my diary that my Dad asked me on my return that, as I had earned so much money working during my industrial placement year at the aerospace company, how was I fixed for money during my final 4th year of my degree. Trouble is I had spent it all, despite the advantageous exchange rate, on my adventures. Everything and some on top thanks to Barclaycard. It was going to be tougher year financially than I planned for perhaps. I still had my student grant from the government. Plus, the expense allowance and book purchase contributions from the aerospace company I was apprenticed with. Just to put that aspect into financial perspective, my government grant was £365 per term for 3 terms, which was equivalent to about £1900 x 3 in 2020. There were no course fees to pay in those days, so after taking off my £12 per week rent x 30 weeks [£360], I had £1,540 left which worked out at £51 per week to cover water, rates, TV license, electricity and gas bills, car tax, insurance, fuel, socialising and, oh yes, nearly forgot, food. That's equivalent to about £260 per week in 2020. So that was ok. There were no mobile phones, Netflix, or satellite TV subscription to pay for in those days. Trouble was my home County Council were notoriously late paying out their grant cheques and it was usually weeks into term time before it arrived. Still my bank, Barclays, were flexible, and they gave me an overdraft facility to supplement my Barclaycard. The interest rate was high, but it evened out the cash flow problem.

Just to be clear though my Dad did help me financially throughout the year and even gave me his previous car when he purchased another one, which was very kind of him. I hardly ran the car though, mainly walking 40 minutes instead to lectures and back every day from my "digs".

Well, that's my story of the incredible action-packed weeks I spent in southern Africa in 1979. Hope you "enjoyed" reading it. What did I learn from my adventures? Looking back now at 1979 from where I am in 2022, I will say this. I don't look back at my life generally and think "wow, that was a great IT strategy I did for such and such a organisation", or "wasn't that a great system implementation I did for so and so". Yes, they were achievements, no denying that, proud of them, but the happiest memories are like the ones I have recorded here. You know …. the ones that bring a smile on your face when you think about them. There's more to life than career and work. Family, yes of course, but also adventure, pushing the boundaries, taking risks, as well as doing good by others, making a difference in some way, that's it. But then again work provides the money to enable just about everything else and "career" gives a sense of achievement, especially if, like me, you were doing something professionally you enjoyed. So, there is no avoiding the need to work for most. Win the lottery? Ok, more likely to be run over by a bus. Wouldn't bank on it. My "prescription" is "hard work, getting back up and carrying on when you get knocked back, resilience and dogged determination".

When I think about the places I visited in Africa I especially recall the many interesting and generous people I met; their diversity; the towns and cties and those special places with little or no human habitation, like the Highveld and Namib Desert. The Milky Way was special too, visible in all its glory at night in Namibia,. Last, but not least by a country mile, the incredibly generosity of Jenny and David for putting me up and, of course, putting up with me for the time I was there with them. Can't have been easy. Thank you.

When I look back at what I did, at the time I did it and the way I did it, and the vast distances I travelled, including into two "war zones", there's only one conclusion I can draw. Regrets? None. I considered my adventures in Southern Africa as an investment in life and memories, not a cost. I was operating quite happily at the extreme end of the "hitch hiking risk spectrum". That makes me "unusual" doesn't it? Hitch hiking around countries like those in 1979 southern Africa is not an experience everyone would relish, is it? Would you?

I took some incredible risks, yes and, this is the important part, got away with it. Would you classify me as a totally bonkers risk taking, adrenaline junkie? Or, perhaps an intrepid, resilient, "can do", adventurer and lover of life, with a thirst for exploration and real adventure? Or just totally bonkers? You will no doubt have drawn your own conclusions, probably somewhere along that spectrum. Let me know if you like. Personally, I've concluded that I'm just wired up differently from most "sensible" people. The risks I took, in exchange for the many incredible experiences I had, would be unacceptable to most, would they not? What would you have done?

My adventures also left an indelible impression on my sense of "identity". It's true what you might have heard, at least in my case anyway. Once you have had been to Africa it gets under your skin, forever. I felt like part of me "belonged" there, like I became part "African". Of course, I only wandered around a small portion of the whole continent and saw some of the rest from 36,000 feet, but the vastness and variety of the areas I did explore can be difficult to comprehend or shake off until you have been there. The place is so huge and varied. The sun, the bright colours, varied smells, people, wildlife, fauna, food, drink and, of course, its rich culture and history. So, when news comes on the TV, even today, about South Africa, Zimbabwe, Eswatini, or Namibia my ears perk up and I listen. It's as if I'm listening to something of importance that is happening in my home country.

So, if I give you a little example of what I mean. I watched the 2009 film "Invictus", starring Matt Damon as Francois Pienaar, the Springboks South African Rugby team captain, and Morgan Freeman as Nelson Mandela. It was about how Mandela used the opportunity of the 1995 Rugby World Cup to bring, what is now often referred to as the "Rainbow Nation", closer together. I couldn't help feeling quite proud about his statesman approach to the transition from the Apartheid era to the Rainbow Nation as I watched, as if it was happening in my own country. I was delighted with the happy ending when South Africa won the cup, but also with the unifying effect that had, bringing the various racial groups closer together.

17. THE SEQUEL

That sense of connection led to a yearning to return and a promise to myself that I would. So, I chose to celebrate a major birthday milestone in 2017 by going back. This time I chose an extensive guided tour from a company with an excellent reputation. A guided tour offered greater safety and certainly over a self-drive holiday…. or hitch hiking, plus it promised a wide variety of experiences and events guided by "experts". Besides my wife was coming along and her idea of fun definitely wasn't a holiday that adopted a DIY approach. To read about that, check out my sequel: "South African, 2017", much of which compares the South Africa I saw in 1979 with the much changed one of 2017.

THE END ……. WELL ALMOST.

This story has been recalled from a mix of memory, diary entries, letters home, which the recipient fortunately kept, and notes taken at the time.

In case you are wondering, the names of key characters in this story have been changed and all surnames and home addresses have been omitted.

ABOUT THE AUTHOR

Keith Richardson was born and grew up in the county of Cumberland in North West England. He was fortunate to have parents who understood the benefit of a good education and fostering a spirit of adventure.

Part of his degree course included a one-year industrial placement, which he spent as a Commercial Apprentice at an aerospace company. The income from that, plus savings from previously working 12 hour shifts in an open cast coal mine and as a barman, enabled him to save enough money to go on this amazing hitch-hiking adventure around South Africa, Swaziland (Eswatini), South West Africa (Namibia) and Zimbabwe-Rhodesia (Zimbabwe).

Retirement, the Coronavirus Pandemic "lockdown periods" of enforced isolation, (2020-2022,) and re-discovery of a box of letters, a diary, papers, and photographs from 1979, presented him with the opportunity to write and reminisce.

Printed in Great Britain
by Amazon

87410546R00088